The Hospitality Edge

Stories to Delight Your Guests, Spark Your Culture and Ignite Productivity

Michael Fiato

TITLE: The Hospitality Edge
By Michael Fiato
Editor Alison Lambert
Contributor Angee Costa
Cover Design Oliver Sunier

Copyright 2020

The author has made every effort possible to check and ensure the accuracy of the information presented in this book. However, the information herein is sold without warranty, either expressed or implied. The author, publisher, nor any dealer or distributor of this book will be held liable for any damages caused either directly or indirectly by the instructions or information contained in this book.

In accordance with the U.S. Copyright Act of 1976, the scanning, uploading, and electronic sharing of any part of this book without the permission of the publisher is unlawful piracy and theft of the author's intellectual property. If you would like to use material from this book (other than for review purposes), prior written permission must be obtained by contacting the publisher. Thank you for your support of the author's rights.

Notice of Rights: All rights reserved. No part of this book may be reproduced or transmitted in any form by any means, electronic, mechanical, photocopy, recording or other without the prior written permission of the publisher.

Permission: For information on getting permission for reprints and excerpts, contact:

Michael Fiato
262 NW Lincoln Circle N
ST Petersburg FL 33702

This book is dedicated to my two partners in adventure:
My Mom – She has taught me to see the best in everything and to have faith.
My Wife Kristen – The Love of my life and the kindest person I have ever met.
Looking forward to what we do next.

Table of Contents

Foreword i

Chapter 1 Connecting on an Emotional Level 1

Chapter 2 Developing Brand Ambassadors 14

Chapter 3 Active Listening 24

Chapter 4 Choosing the Right People 36

Chapter 5 Investing in the Right People 46

Chapter 6 "Show Time" Behaviors 60

Chapter 7 Service Recovery 70

Chapter 8 Developing a Dynamic Team 84

Chapter 9 Collaboration & Accountability 108

Conclusion 116

Foreword

Wanting to follow my passion for cooking. I started my career in hotels and country clubs. At age 27, I decided to open my own restaurant, Michaels Café. I was a chef, and it was truly the only thing I ever wanted to do. I was in my second year when a much-needed family trip to Walt Disney World changed everything. At the time, my restaurant was booming and I was exhausted. I believe that trip was the first time I had two days off back-to-back since we opened.

I don't have any children; but I do have a niece. Sadly, she could not go on the trip, so I bought a huge Mickey Mouse doll to take home to her when the trip was over. On the first day, my wife Kristen and I left Mickey in the hotel room sitting on a chair and headed out for a day of fun in the park. When we returned, I noticed Mickey was not where we left him. Now, he was sitting on the bed with a soda in one hand, the remote in the other, and he was watching TV. I have seen movies where dolls come alive, and those stories don't usually end well. Luckily, our Mickey was not alive or possessed. Our housekeeper had cleaned our room, and just to amuse and entertain us, had left him in that new position. I thought it was nearly the coolest thing I had ever seen.

On the second day of the vacation, we headed over to Epcot. Even though Epcot has some of the most mind-blowing attractions in the world, I could not stop thinking about my hotel room. I was a bit distracted, wondering what Mickey was going to be doing upon our return. I dismissed those thoughts thinking the housekeeper probably only had one trick, and I had seen it already with the soda can and the remote. But I had a lot to learn about hospitality that extends far above and beyond expectations. When we returned, Mickey was standing on the desk, fully decked out in my workout clothes looking like he was getting ready for a run. By the way, my clothes were too big for him he looked ridiculous. I loved it!

> "People will forget what you said and forget what you did; but people will never forget how you made them feel."
>
> *Maya Angelou*

On our final day, I was totally distracted. I was having a blast on the trip, but from time to time, my mind wandered and I couldn't help but thinking, 'What will Mickey be doing today?' I kept looking at my watch, waiting for the time to come for my return to the hotel room. Finally, it was time. I opened the door, ran into the room and saw that Mickey was … gone! Immediately I thought, 'The housekeeper stole my mouse! I thought this was the happiest place on earth? This could not possibly be the way this story ends!' So, I started to search the room in the desperate hope that I hadn't been robbed. I looked in the closet, and Mickey was not there. I dropped to the floor to look under the bed. No Mickey. Now, I was mad and resolved to march down to the front desk and get this housekeeper fired. I stormed through the room toward the exit. As I passed the bathroom, I noticed the "do not disturb" sign on the bathroom door. I chuckled and wondered what Mickey could be doing in there, as I slowly turned the doorknob. Sure enough, Mickey was in the tub with a bar of soap in his hand and a shower cap on his head. Wow!

I learned during that trip what Super Bowl MVP, Roger Staubach, meant when he said, "There are no traffic jams along the extra mile." I was so enamored by something so simple, yet so brilliant, and it opened up a world that I did not know existed—the world of hospitality. Disney had found a way to make something as ordinary and mundane as walking into your hotel room a thing of wonder and great anticipation. I was stunned by the experience. After all, I know how hard being a housekeeper is, yet somehow this person understood that their job was not solely to clean my room. Cleaning my room was a task that needed

> "Do what you do so well that they will want to see it again and bring their friends."
>
> Walt Disney

to be completed to get to the greater purpose – creating a memory. They took an ordinary and unpleasant task and spun it into gold, creating memories for me and my family that we will never forget.

That experience ran through my mind, and I could not let it go. Finally, after some thought, I told my wife that I wanted to sell the restaurant and devote the rest of my career to doing this.

My wife was quite sure that I had lost my mind. "You want to pose dolls around hotel rooms?" she asked nervously. "No," I assured her. "I want to make people feel what that housekeeper made me feel."

I knew that my life had undergone a major shift. When we returned from the trip, I sold the restaurant and began to work with frontline teams to create amazing experiences for their guests. My goal was to create work environments that inspired team members to bring the best version of themselves to work every day, and to love what they do. Hospitality can change your life; it certainly changed mine.

When you consider the word hospitality, you can't help but notice the similarity to the word 'hospital.' The two concepts don't seem related. But a closer look at the origin of the word reveals that they are etymological cousins. The origin of both words is the Latin word *hospes*, which means to have power.

> "Only a life lived to the service of others is worth living."
>
> Albert Einstein

The word is not limited to customer service, good business, or receiving guests in your home. Instead, its specific connotation is 'taking care of guests who are far away from their homes' as you would in a hospital, hotel, or even a hostel. The earliest instances of the word *hospes* refer to people who came to visit your home from afar. They were called *hospes*. But let's return to that meaning, to have power. When people are visiting your hotel, restaurant, theme park, theater, etc., you really do have the power to make that experience memorable in both positive and negative ways. As they enter your place of business, they are in your hands, so to speak, and it is up to you to decide if they will feel warm and welcomed or disregarded and ignored.

As we will explore, hospitality is quite different from customer service, it's an elevated experience. You'll notice that I use the term *'guest'* versus 'customer' in many of my stories, and that's because the word customer has a minimal, transactional feel, while the word guest elevates the expectation of the interaction. It connects more to the emotions people experience when they do business with you. It is impossible to separate emotions from commerce. It is a critical part of the experience. So, it is critical to tap into the most positive emotions, which leaves no room for the typical anxiety people experience when they travel, shop, or dine. These important hospitality encounters are not just good—or even great. They are memorable. They are over-the-top. They place a high value on the guest that typical service can't touch.

As we elevate the guest experience, we should also use the correct terms when referring to your team. Please avoid the terms "staff," "associate," and "human capital." All three terms are dreadful and do not represent the people who create the magic every day. I like the terms "team" and "team members," because I recognize that without the team, I am nowhere.

In a Forbes magazine article, senior contributor, Micah Solomon, shares an amazing story of outstanding hospitality in the hotel industry as witnessed by hospitality expert, Jay Coldren: "A couple arrived at the Inn from Pittsburgh, four hours away, to celebrate their anniversary with a three-night stay. As the team members unloaded the luggage, our female guest said to her husband, "Don't forget my hanging bag." Her husband looked into the truck and came up with a horrified expression on his face. He had left her bag beside the car in their garage. This poor woman was checking into one of the most expensive places on the planet with nothing but the clothes on her back. One of the team members drove up to the front of the inn in the company car. He smiled and said, "Get me their keys and the address." I was floored. No one asked him to do this. He was so much a part of the service culture that he knew the exact right thing to do. He drove eight hours straight and made it back before their dinner reservations at nine."

What is it that makes an organization rise to such heights of service? I believe it is the culture of service that is carefully crafted by management. Team members are empowered to make the guest smile—just as the origin of the word "hospitality" implies. They have the power to act in the guest's best interest. And, they reap the rewards of guests who are wowed and amazed. These are not one-off experiences. It is a full paradigm shift that makes the customer truly a guest and the employee a host that cares for them.

Buzzwords in hospitality are not rare. Concepts like "return on investment," "hosting," and "productivity" have swirled around the industry for years. In fact, the word hospitality itself has devolved into a buzzword that people do not glean deep meaning from. Managers have gotten so caught up in the process of measuring metrics and key performance indicators that they lost touch with the core of their business: people. Those people they were supposed to be concerned for included both their team and their guests.

But, as the hospitality industry changed, its customer base changed right along with it. Guests demanded a higher base level of service, making it more difficult to exceed their already high expectations. The power shifted from the company to the guest. Team members were told that "the customer is always right," but now they believed it, raising the bar for all hospitality and service industries. And because our economy is so global, the service you provide is no longer only measured against the service provided by your competitors, but also against all other service providers everywhere.

Guests know that they have a voice that they did not have before. One guest has an incredible amount of reach. Gone are the days of the neighborhood store where a bad experience was shared with family and a neighbor or two. Today's guest can reach the other side of the world, and everywhere in between, thanks to easy access wireless internet and the thousands of social media connections available right in their pockets. Sociologist Tim Elmore estimates that "the most introverted of people will influence 10,000 others in an average lifetime." Guests are powerful, opinionated, and well-connected. How do you satisfy a guest like that? More importantly, how do you amaze them?

People are incredibly imaginative and creative. Just like the housekeeper and the mouse, given the right environment, they can figure out ways to make the humans they serve experience emotion they did not expect to feel when doing business with them. Many people incorrectly assume that Chick-fil-A employees are trained to say, "My pleasure," rather than, "You're welcome" in response to a thank you. The truth is that the instruction to say, "My pleasure," does not appear in any Chick-fil-A manual. It caught on after the company's founder, Truett Cathy, remarked at how nice it was to hear the phrase when he visited an upscale hotel chain. It spread like wildfire and all team members adopted the practice as a part of the company culture.

It turns out that much of what makes hospitality next-level is how you make a guest feel about the service you deliver. It is cultural. True hospitality is not an empty or vague concept. It cannot be reduced to a buzzword. It is a rich tapestry woven by a million little touches that let them know they are an honored guest. It revolves around a level of freedom the team has, not only to meet the guest's needs, but to surprise them in unforgettable ways. Whoever said, "Don't sweat the small stuff," really missed the mark. Hospitality is all about the details; the small stuff is what counts.

Chapter 1

Connecting on an Emotional Level

I have a confession to make—I drink a lot of coffee. In fact, I can easily drink around 14 cups a day whether I need it or not. I also do not care very much about where the coffee comes from. I love coffee so much, I will drink airplane coffee and that awful hotel coffee. You are just as likely to see me sipping java at Starbucks, Dunkin Donuts, or Caribou. In fact, I will even drink vending machine coffee if there is no other alternative.

I travel for work and often my location often dictates the source of my coffee. When I am home, I can choose which coffee shop I will visit. Right across the street, just 300 yards from my house, there is a large chain donut store that serves a perfectly good cup of coffee. I could literally walk across the street in my pajamas and get a cup there. But that is not where I go when I have the choice. Instead, I jump in my car, burn the time and gas to drive 7.5 miles to a high-end coffee shop. Keep in mind that I am the guy who will down vending machine coffee like it is a fancy cappuccino. I don't necessarily like the boutique coffee house's blend better than the cheap chain's fare.

And, I certainly do not enjoy spending the mind-numbing $5 they charge me. So, why do I choose to make the drive to the other place?

It's the way they treat me. That's it! That's why I go. The barista, Nicole, knows my name. And, obviously, I know hers. She remembers that I travel for a living. On Mondays, she draws a little plane on my cup and writes, "Have a great week!" to send me off on my next trip. When I return on Fridays, she always writes, "Welcome back!" I almost never have to place an order because when they see my car pull up, they start making my usual. On weekends, they make my wife's coffee without even asking. It's like walking onto the set of "Cheers," and it proves that people are drawn to places where everybody knows your name.

Contrast that to the donut chain conveniently located just across the street from home. I have been in there a few times—certainly enough times for them to recognize me. But they don't know my name, they don't know my order, and they never seem happy to see me. I feel like an interruption to whatever it is they are doing. Every time I go in there, a different team is working, indicating that the turnover is exceptionally high. Are you surprised?

> "A man without a smiling face must not open a shop."
>
> *Chinese Proverb*

At the boutique coffee house, turnover is not a major issue. Sure, people leave. But Nicole and her team have been together for years;

they are a well-oiled machine. But, more importantly, they love what they do! It is fun to watch them work because they truly seem to enjoy their jobs, as well as their guests. They bring the best version of themselves to work every day. And, they keep me coming back, despite the distance and the cost. I pay $1 for the drink, but I pay the other $4 for the experience.

If you ask the average person what hospitality means, they will be able to answer you with relative ease. But when your business is people, hospitality must be so much more than just "treating others nicely or welcoming them to your home or business." It moves from the realm of good to great.

Hospitality guru and founder of Union Square Hospitality Group, Danny Meyer, said, "You may think, as I once did, that I'm primarily in the business of serving good food. Actually, though, food is secondary to something that matters even more. In the end, what's most meaningful is creating positive, uplifting outcomes for human experiences and human relationships. Business, like life, is all about how you make people feel. It's that simple, and it's that hard."

Creating a great guest experience is challenging. But it is not rocket science. It goes back to the golden rule, "Do unto others as you would have them do unto you." But exceptional hospitality is personified in the platinum rule: "Do unto others as they would be done unto." We have all had good guest experiences, as well as unpleasant ones. We know the difference. But to bring those concepts to life, we have to be intentional about the precious moments we spend with our guests.

There is a simple fact in business, regardless of what business you're in. Businesses that connect with their guests on an emotional level enjoy unprecedented success. It can be easy to miss, but certain brands drive a level of emotion that inspires guests to declare their love for them. Seriously! It is that love that rises out of the interaction with customers. The difference between hospitality and other levels of service is that hospitality is the only one that is driven primarily by emotion. People often debate the best quality in a leader. Many answers arise, but among them is the concept of empathy. Empathy is deeply emotional connection. Much like hospitality, when leadership touches people in an emotional way, it rises to a level that is hard to beat. And, because of the emotional aspect of hospitality, everyone needs it, whether they know it or not. They will feel uneasy when it isn't there, even if they cannot articulate exactly what was missing in their interaction with your business.

It is the same reason why the Apple Store is always the busiest store in any mall. Of course, the products Apple sells are amazing. But the way the employees make you feel about traveling across town and spending your hard-earned dollars is what we really crave. As a brand, Apple makes their guests feel superior, which for many people is worth nearly as much as the new tech they're after! And why does Starbucks always have a line of guests patiently waiting for their morning coffee? It's because we feel like the decision to buy our coffee from there was a smart one. We feel like we are in the know, a member of the club, and bright enough to crack the code. Or what about the salesman who wears an expensive suit during the week, then changes out of his professional threads and dons a leather jacket on the weekends to ride his motorcycle and proudly display his Harley Davidson tattoo? He is passionate about this great motorcycle brand because of the emotional connection he's built with the business. This connection says as much about the guest as it does about the companies we patronize. We feel like insiders. We feel like family.

The why is simple: These brands have connected with their guests at an emotional level. Their products have become more than something we want. They are something we need because they help to define who we are and what we are about. And only that specific brand will do. These guests are brand ambassadors promoting the brand to everyone.

Hospitality takes the clay of a great product or service and molds it into a thing of beauty that is presented to the discriminating guest as a prize. It is the great differentiator in business.

Danny Meyer often speaks of the Hospitality Quotient. It a simple concept that breaks up the guest service component of business into two parts: Technical and Emotional.

Technical Service is best described as the nuts and bolts of every business. Are you open on time? Is the food hot? Are your shelves full? Is your store clean? Are the employees neatly dressed, well-groomed, and in uniform? Do employees say 'please' and 'thank you?' All of these are critical parts of the guest experience. Miss any of them and your guests will rain their displeasure on your company. The technical piece of service is both critical and non-negotiable. It is a basic expectation your guests have when they walk in the door. It is the most foundational part of the unwritten transactional contract between patron and merchant. They are counting on you to get all of these pieces right.

The challenge, though, is that no one makes a decision based on technical service. You don't choose a restaurant or retailer on those aspects of service because you expect to see them everywhere you go. If a merchant fails to deliver on the basics, they will soon have to lock the doors and take the signs down. Sadly, you don't get any special congratulations for getting the basics right. Think about it: When you and your spouse chose a restaurant to visit for your 25th wedding anniversary, did you make your choice simply because the place had great air conditioning? Most likely not. You wanted an experience that matched the importance of the event.

What you were after—what all guests want—is the emotional experience that stellar hospitality delivers. The heart of the matter is simply this: Guests choose to visit one place over another based on how those places make them feel. And that is the emotional side of service. Positive emotion connects you and your team to your guests.

Whoever said, "Don't sweat the small stuff," did not run a successful business. It turns out that the small stuff is huge stuff! It is the stuff that connects a guest to your business.

A smile, for example, is an irresistible gesture that even the crabbiest guest cannot defy. Yet, in many companies, the sight of an employee offering a genuine smile to a customer is as rare as a sighting of the Loch Ness monster. The emotions a smile invokes include joy, comfort, and inclusion. If you doubt the power of emotion in business, you can see its effects when hospitality is missing and the guest interaction goes poorly. Guests can become outraged to the point of screaming when they feel the merchant has not held up his or her end of the invisible social contract. You might remember the guest who called 911 because her neighborhood McDonald's ran out of chicken nuggets. That level of emotion is admittedly bordering on insane. But if you've even been on the receiving end of an angry guest, you would admit that emotions are a part of the transaction.

Our goal is to channel all of the emotion—that of the guest and of the team—in the most positive direction to produce an experience both will find gratifying and enriching.

When we receive amazing hospitality, it communicates several very powerful messages:

I see you.

When a guest walks into a busy hotel, restaurant, or other service industry establishment, they are immediately aware of the fact that they are one of many other guests demanding the time and attention of the team. It is easy for them to worry that they will be overlooked. When every team member stops and makes eye contact with that guest just to smile and say hello, that anxiety subsides. It communicates to the guest that the company is not too busy to notice them and make them feel welcomed.

I want to hear from you.

Making eye contact and listening intently to every guest communicates that we want to hear what they have to say, whether it is a service request or the story of something that just happened on their long flight from Seattle. Taking time to listen taps into that innate emotional need we all have to be heard. At the Fish Market in Seattle, they stress to "Be Present" with guests. In that 2-3 minute exchange, it's like being with a good friend; you are fully present, making eye contact and actively listening. You are there.

I care about you.

Going out of your way to do something special—something unexpected—tells the guest that you care about them. It tells them that he or she matters beyond the basics of what they paid for, like a hotel room or a theater ticket. It also gives any team member an opportunity to fully engage in the emotions of the guest. When the team are engaged, they want to give their all. They want to draw out that smile or the gasp that comes from exceeding the guests' expectations. That creates a feedback loop where guests praise the team and the team keeps producing more praise-worth results.

I want to take care of you.

Let's face it, when guests patronize us, they are taking a risk. The food may not be good. The hotel room might be dirty. The ride might break down. The Teams who are empowered to care for their guests are anxious to take a problem and turn it into an opportunity to shine. The team become the super heroes flying around, meeting needs, and building loyalties that last a lifetime.

When guests and team members connect on an emotional level, it changes the content of their conversation. They begin to talk about in terms of how they feel. Of course, the effects are felt in the bottom line. But the motivation supersedes money. The money is simply a barometer of how well the job of hospitality is able to meet guests on that emotional level.

It is seen in the hotel that greets every guest immediately with a broad smile and a sincere welcome, the bartender who remembers your favorite drink and makes it just the way you like it, and the home décor retailer that walks with you throughout the buying experience helping you choose fabrics, colors, and textures that you love. They all understand the heart of the matter. When you leave their presence, you take with you a feeling that keeps you coming back for more.

In Hospitality Magazine, Hotel Solutions Associate, Mark Godfrey, writes:

> *Businesses across all sectors have been realizing that it is relatively easy to replicate the physical offering of their competitors, so the battleground has moved to the 'emotional' experience, which is not so easy to replicate. Initial research into the importance of emotions in an experience, has been undertaken by a UK-based consultancy firm called Beyond Philosophy. It suggests that emotions account for over 50% of the total experience. More recently, another consultancy suggested this figure is now 70%. So clearly, in the hospitality industry we ignore emotions at our peril...*
>
> *We have long subscribed to the mantra of 'recruit for attitude, train for skills'. Hire people who love to serve guests and then train them in the technical skills to do their jobs well.... Colleagues also want to feel valued and cared for, so they need good leadership, to feel supported in their roles, to*

be empowered to deliver great service and to be coached and mentored constantly. Good communication is vital as colleagues like to know what is going on and feel involved with the business… Emotions are an area that traditionally we have not given a lot of consideration in hospitality, but as they become increasingly important, now is the time to start thinking about how you can create more positive emotional experiences for your guests.

Hospitality, for a company, is like a mirror: You will always get back exactly what you give. Smiles are contagious and guests want to do business in a place that makes them feel special. And they want to know that the team cares about the things they care about. Often, especially in the hotel industry, people are visiting while under varying levels of stress. Perhaps they are in their fourth city in as many weeks and are weary from the constant travel. They may be traveling to visit a sick relative. It may be a positive reason that brought them in, but the stress of being away from home leaving family, pets, or just the familiar behind weighs on them. We have all joked that we need a vacation after our vacation due to the high stress that comes with being away from home. The same is true in most service situations. Even a night out with a spouse can get stressful if we fear we've chosen the wrong restaurant, evidenced by the fact that no one greeted us at the door, the wait was eternal with no apology, and the server rushed us through our ordering process to get to the next table.

Stories of amazing tales of hospitality abound in companies where the culture is primed and prepped for such magic to occur. Accor Hotels empowers its employee to make guests' experiences memorable by using an interesting technique. After check-in, agents have been known to look the guest up on social media to find out what kinds of things they like, and then send a gift to the guest's room that would be meaningful to them.

Nancy Trejos of USA Today gave examples of how Accor Hotels has surprised their guests all over the world. For the guest who likes fine dining, an all-day behind-the-scenes tour of Tru in Chicago, along with a night at the Sofitel Chicago Water Tower. For the guest who likes fishing, an eco-friendly fishing trip in the San Diego Bay. For the guest who likes luxury cars, a certificate to drive a Ferrari and Lamborghini. For the guest who likes lounging in spas, a day at the Hela spa in Washington, D.C., plus an overnight stay at the Sofitel. And for the guest who likes sports, VIP tickets to a hockey game between the San Jose Sharks and the Red Wings.

Imagine the emotional response of guests upon receiving such a specialized gift, just for doing business with the company. And think of how vested each employee becomes after doing their research to find the perfect gift for their guests. When the guests pour out their praise on the team, it deepens the love for the job of serving others.

Chapter 2
Developing Brand Ambassadors

Andy Hasselman writes for the website, Think in 3D, where he shares the story of Joshie the Giraffe. It seems Andy has always been impressed with the hospitality philosophy of The Ritz Carlton, which famously empowers its team members to spend up to $2,000 to solve a guest problem or simply to make a guest feel valued. They can spend those funds completely at their own discretion with no approval needed from a manager. It seems, according to Andy, that a little boy staying with his family at The Ritz Carlton at Amelia Island left behind a treasured family toy: a stuffed animal who answered to the name Joshie. Chris was understandably frantic at the loss of his constant companion with whom he slept every single night. Thankfully, Joshie was later discovered by the team. He had made it into a laundry hamper but had come through the wash and dry cycles just fine. The hospitality team contacted the family, who by now had returned home, to let them know that Joshie was safe and on his way back to them.

Chris' dad thanked the team, advising them that he had calmed his son's fears by telling him that Joshie was having a few extra days' vacation. But, before returning Joshie, the team members had a brilliant idea. Capitalizing on dad's words of comfort to little Chris, they positioned the little stuffie all around the hotel having the time of his life. Photos of Joshie riding in a golf cart, lounging by the pool, getting a massage, running hotel security, and hanging out with a collection of other stuffed friends delighted the family beyond words. After such an experience, can you imagine that family will stay in any other hotel when they are travelling to the Florida area? I think not.

What made all of this possible was the amazing team at the Ritz-Carlton. Consider all of the people who had to work in tandem to create this experience for the family. It required a laundry team that was alert and conscientious enough to find someone in Loss Prevention who could investigate the situation. The Loss Prevention Team then had to work with teams all over the hotel, including the golf course attendants, masseuse, and security team to create the amazing photos of Joshie having a blast at the Ritz.

Empowerment has become quite a buzzword. It is used to describe everything from social justice statements to relationship philosophy. But in the hospitality industry, empowerment exceeds mere jargon. It is the stuff of hospitality legends. And it is a mindset shift in what makes a worker much more than an employee, and elevates them to the regal status of brand ambassador.

Many companies employ brand ambassadors. These are people hired to get the public talking about the company and helping to generate interest in what it offers. They are supposed to be the ultimate advocates of the company's image to the marketplace. But hiring someone for the job of brand ambassador is far different from creating a corporate culture where every team member operates in that mode. To achieve that, companies must establish a few key top-down philosophies that ensure every employee is motivated and incentivized to represent the company in stellar fashion every day. Here are just a few of those critical philosophies:

> "People will work for a living but they will die for recognition."
>
> Unknown

Your Teammates are your most valuable commodity.

The landscape is littered with companies that claim to put their people first. Truth be told, very few companies actual do it. True empowerment inspires the imagination it takes to perform like those amazing Ritz-Carlton employees did. Imagine if Joshie had been found by a team member who had been forced to work overtime on her daughter's 13th birthday, resulting in her missing the birthday party. Do you think that team member would care to make an unforgettable experience for the guest? Not likely. Poor Joshie might have ended up on the trash heap rather than on a massage table being pampered by the hotel's finest. A Gallup Poll found that disgruntled, neglected, and disengaged employees cost companies billions of dollars every year in low performance, turnover, and absenteeism. But despite compelling evidence to the contrary, companies continue to place employee engagement low on the totem pole.

A healthy and positive culture goes a long way toward rocketing team engagement and ensuring **internal service**. External service, the kind that is focused on the guest, is only as effective as the company's ability to grow internal service, the kind focused on the company's internal team members. Each team member is a kind of a guest. They are guests of the company and of each other. By generating an atmosphere where the team know that they are the greatest asset the company has, it can ensure that they come to work for far more than a paycheck.

> "Train people well enough so they can leave; treat them well enough so they don't want to."
>
> *Richard Branson*

The old joke says, "Employees work just hard enough to not get fired, and companies pay just enough that they don't quit." This is a poor paradigm and results in average performance at best.

Employees need roots and wings.

The best brand ambassador are those team members who are firmly rooted in the company's philosophy, but who have been given the freedom and elasticity to flex their own hospitality muscles in the care of their guests. Let's unpack that concept a bit.

Roots refers to the training the team receives both at onboarding and throughout his or her career with the company. During the onboarding process, the team gets their first real taste of the spirit of the company. They get to see who the leadership is and discover what environment will surround them for the next several years of their working life. That is the best time to begin the process of letting the team know that he or she is the most valuable asset the company has. It is also the best time to set the expectations for how the team are to represent the brand for which they are working. Furthermore, throughout the teams' career, the messaging restating and reaffirming company values helps to solidify the understanding that hospitality is the prime objective. Companies should prioritize the team so that they can prioritize their guests.

Employees need ownership and autonomy.

One of the best ways to foster a spirit of brand ambassadorship is to provide the team with boundaries in which they can operate to immediately care for a guest. We have all been in the grocery store when the register rang $2.99 for an item that was $1.99. We may have even pointed out the over-charge to the cashier. But this is where the nightmare begins. The cashier needs to contact a manager, a process that seems to take forever. It is almost as if the manager is stuck at the top of a snowy mountain and must trek down through a blizzard to make it your register to resolve the issue. The manager must then hear about the problem as retold by the cashier. Then the manager must investigate to determine what the price should be by trotting over to aisle to check the shelf tag or by sending a distracted and unmotivated junior employee to do so. By the time the CSI-style investigation is complete, the line is shooting daggers behind you for holding them all up with your little problem. Once the manager determines that you are, indeed, correct about the price discrepancy, he or she must swipe the magic card that allows the price change so that the transaction can continue.

    If you calculated the wasted time of everything involved that was spent waiting for the manager to arrive, not to mention the mounting frustration of the guests waiting behind you, the cost is far more than the $1 that was being investigated. If the store had simply hired amazing cashiers they could trust and had given them the authority to resolve the conflict quickly, they would have created a more positive experience for everyone involved and saved the $1. What's more, they would have taken one small step toward greater guest loyalty for you and everyone in line watching their stellar hospitality.

Giving employee freedom to act on the guests' behalf gives them a sense of pride and fosters strong relationships between guests and the team that keeps guest coming back.

Show your team how much you care.

Here again, the emotional side of leadership and business is paramount. Your team wants to feel respected, valued, and yes, even loved. They want to be treated with dignity, kindness, patience, and empathy. It needs to be more than words on a page or a training module on a screen. It needs to flow through the lifeblood of the organization. Inauthentic, canned, and impotent corporate slogans about how much a company appreciates its team members are useless. People are excellent judges of character, whether or not they act on their better judgement. They can smell a farce a mile away. Corporate empathy and concern for its employees must be genuine and prompted by a clear understanding that without the team, there is no company. Let's be honest: no matter how luxurious the hotel or how posh the restaurant, if there aren't caring team there to greet guests, escort them to various locations, serve them, and respond to their needs, the doors would be locked and the windows boarded. It's all about the team.

A great way to communicate to your team how much you care is by establishing a relentless recognition program. Recognition should take place at every gathering, both large and small. Everything from a pat on the back and a quick, "Great job!" as you pass a high performer's desk, to a grand company celebration complete with awards, are all effective in letting the team know they matter. Personally I really like sending a personal note – it's powerful and genuine. Think back to the way you felt the last time you received a hand-written thank you note.

This kind of paradigm shift makes sense. But it also makes dollars. Studies have proven again and again that high levels of employee satisfaction result in more frequent and higher guest survey rankings. And happy employees have a direct impact on the bottom line.

The old adage "praise in public, punish in private" proves to be accurate. The team needs to hear managers say their names publicly while praising their excellent performance. Guest reviews need to be read aloud rather than posted on some obscure bulletin next to the breakroom. Guest praise should generate applause for the employee who went above and beyond the call of duty to amaze a guest. It should be posted prominently in company ads, emails, and in every meeting.

"You're going to like the way you look. I guarantee it."

My early hospitality journey put me in touch with some truly innovative companies and amazing leaders. One of my favorite interactions involved Men's Warehouse and George Zimmer. My career was progressing and my CEO let me know that my wardrobe needed an upgrade. There was a Men's Warehouse close by, so I thought it was a great place to start. I knew of them and had read about the founder, George Zimmer. They had the most unique radio and TV ads. Most started with a guest calling George and recalling a great experience they had in his store. The guest would always name the city and the Men's Warehouse associate by name. George closed each ad with his signature, "You will love the way you look. I guarantee it!"

My personal experiences with the local Men's Warehouse team were always excellent. The sales team provided personal attention, they had great product knowledge, and they always listened to me. I got in the habit of visiting their stores while I traveled because I was interested to see if the experience was as good outside of my local store. It was! The brand hired, onboarded, and trained the sales team really well.

On one of my visits, I had a conversation with a sales associate. I shared how impressed I was and went on to tell my story, my life's mission, and how cool it would be to talk directly to George. The salesmen went to back and came out with a business card. He said, "Here is George's number. Give him a call!"

Well, you better believe that I did! He answered and I recognized his voice right away. We had a great conversation; he was kind and so willing to share. At one point in the conversation, the Men's Warehouse ads came up, along with his signature tagline. This is where it really got interesting. George explained that the ads were designed with two purposes. The first was clear: he wanted new customers and he wanted to sell suits. The second was enlightening:

George wanted the ads to speak directly to his sales team. He wanted to remind them that they owned the experience with every guest and that they were empowered to create great experiences for each one. Most importantly, they were promise keepers, and it was their purpose to make every guest that walked out of their store "like the way they looked." George made sure that those who kept his promise were recognized on national airways. That's pretty powerful!

Chapter 3
Active Listening

The power of listening ranks way up there with the super powers of flying, teleportation, and invisibility. It is a critical life skill and is the heartbeat of any successful hospitality strategy. Meeting your guests' needs depends on your ability to hear those needs—both the spoken and unspoken ones. Guests are always talking to us, even when their lips are not moving. They speak to us through facial expressions, their body movements, and most importantly, in their decision of whether or not to do business with us.

Bitten by the hospitality bug, I got serious about entering this fascinating new world. I was embarking on a fresh era in my life with the confidence that this was the right move for me. With the restaurant gone, I had the time I needed to devour everything I could find on customer service. I started by

> "True hospitality consists of giving the best of yourself to your guests."
>
> *Eleanor Roosevelt*

educating myself and read one book a week. Some of my favorite titles from my time of exploration and discovery were "Fish," "Gung Ho," and "The Disney Way." But I did not discriminate. In a short time, I had read every service book I could find in Barnes & Noble. I also attended trainings and seminars. I was particularly impacted by the training workshops offered by Disney and Zingerman's, and I spent a weekend in Seattle at the famous Pike Place Fish Market, all of which I'll share more about later. To say I was obsessed with the world of hospitality would be an understatement; all of my free time was spent researching and learning. Once I had consumed everything I could, I expanded my study to the fields of psychology and sociology by studying people. I explored everything from how people learn to reading body language and studying consumer behavior. I was the most eager student west of the Mississippi, and I was loving my new pursuit.

I was so engrossed in my studies, it took a gentle nudge from my wife to remind me that I needed to work as well. So, I initiated the search for a job. But I did not want just any position. I was hoping to find something that would provide me the balance I needed and would support this new passion I had developed. I had some exposure to business dining and the Monday through Friday schedule was exactly what I needed.

After some research, I applied to the Big 3: Aramark, Sodexo, and Compass Group. All three companies offered me a job. I chose

Compass Group because they had the best food programs by far, and they were the only company that talked about growth. They also demonstrated a strong commitment to training their people.

I started working as an assistant manager in food service at a large computer company. We were responsible for four buildings where our cafés were located. I was pleasantly surprised at the food quality, and I really enjoyed the speed of service. The level of hospitality wasn't bad, but it was not at the level I was used to from my own restaurant. And it certainly did not meet the standard of all I had learned in my study of the hospitality industry.

Hotels, country clubs, and restaurants put a huge emphasis on gaining new guests and retaining the ones they have. That is not the case in the corporate environment. Companies have a captive audience. Most people will overlook small failures in a café located in their building because of the convenience it offers. So, they tolerate some snags rather than go out to their cars, drive a few miles away, and get lunch elsewhere. Their time is too valuable. But rather than see this group of guests as a given, I instead saw this as a great opportunity to start trying what I had learned, and more importantly, measure the results.

My manager was Tom, a seasoned pro who taught me a management technique I continue to use to this day: "The Colombo." For those of you who have been living under a rock (or those under the age of 30), Colombo was the name of a famous TV Detective from the

70s. His signature move was to complete his conversation with someone, walk away, and then immediately turn around and say, "Just one more thing." In some cases, he would do that multiple times in one conversation. Each time he returned, he would ask a follow-up question that got him deeper and deeper into the murderer's psyche and exasperated the murderer so torturously, they would almost always make some ill-advised move to throw Colombo off their trail. And it would be that move that allowed Colombo to catch them. This is how Tom managed me.

In the morning he would say, "Mike, we need to get the financials in line at building A." I would then get started on that task. A few hours later, Tom would show up and ask me how I was going to do the task. He never gave orders about how something needed to be done; he just listened. When he liked an idea, he would nod in affirmation. If he didn't like an idea, he would tilt his head and ask a follow-up question, forcing me to dig deep into my analytical skills. He might ask, "Why do you think that's the right move?" or "How do you think will that impact the financials?" He never micromanaged me. He simply the used the effective combination of listening carefully and asking follow-up questions until he was aligned with my solution. I never knew at the time if I was brilliantly inventing solutions or if he was brilliantly steering me toward the right solutions. I later learned, of course, it was a combination of the two; he had great ideas he was leading me to, but he also allowed for my good ideas to supersede his own when appropriate.

Initially, this management style was frustrating. It forced me to be introspective, diagnostic, and creative. I had not been managed in a long time and was used to working as I wanted. It took a while for me to understand the genius behind what Tom was doing. My work personality tends to be aggressive. I like to jump in, go with my gut, and fix things. Tom never told me what to do. By asking questions rather than barking out orders, he was slowing me down, guiding me to think through my solutions, and developing me into a better manager. Ultimately, I learned to make better decisions.

Patience and thoughtfulness are necessary attributes of leadership. I thank Tom for skillfully teaching me both. We are still friends to this day and occasionally get to work together.

So, the great news was that we did really well. Our account was the most profitable in the Southeast, we signed a new contract, and we started to sell business. That is when fate struck! A large account right down the street became available and I was interested. Unfortunately, company policy stated that I could not make a move away from my present location until I had been there for at least a year. Tom graciously allowed me to post for the job, but we both knew it was a longshot.

Amazingly, two days later I was offered the job! How awesome was that? I was overjoyed and internally bragged that they must have heard how incredibly skilled I was. I was so full of myself! Later, I learned the truth. This account had the reputation of being a "manager slayer," and it had killed no less than three managers in the prior year. The account never made money, the client was demanding, and the team turnover was the worst in the Southeast. The client expected an internal candidate, and I was the only one who applied. After I heard all of the details, I was still excited. I surmised that this was a perfect opportunity for me to apply what I learned about customer service. I was certain that I was the one who could turn this account around. Boy, was I wrong!

Failure is a funny thing. Even if you have had much of it, you are never quite prepared for it. From the start, everything that could go wrong went terribly wrong. And although I continued to work really hard, it became evident that the culture at this account was broken, and this was not a problem that I could just plow through. It went from bad to worse, and in my third month, the client gave us notice that if we didn't improve in 30 days, we would lose the contract. I shared the news with my District Manager; he was not happy, but also not really surprised. I was pretty sure that the next 30 days would be my last with Compass Group, and they would not retain me.

I informed the team of our situation and headed to my office. My desk was a mess filled with all of my books on hospitality. Additionally, I had my own hospitality platform I was working on, so all of my notes and research were strewn everywhere. A co-worker,

Chef David, came in to discuss the news, took one look at my cluttered desk, and asked, "What's all this stuff?" I explained it was going to be my life's work that I had hoped to implement it in the field someday. I took David through the documents and where I was at with it at the time. He listened intently and asked, "Why don't we do all of that here?" It was a great question, and really, what did I have to lose?

We started the next afternoon with an all-team meeting. We watched "Who Framed Roger Rabbit" for fun. I wanted the team to understand Disney's concept of "Bumping the Lamp," which means going above and beyond what was expected, to create something genuinely great. Then, we discussed the hospitality materials and how we could create great experiences for all of our guests. I asked everyone to make a list of what they would like to see changed and how they would improve our work environment. The suggestions began to fly around the room in an excited frenzy. By the time we were done brainstorming, we had 85 items from our team where we needed to improve. We put them on large flipchart paper and hung them around the kitchen. As we completed items, team members were rewarded. We quickly created a culture of celebrating each other's success. We had trophies and gold medals; it was fun! More importantly, I could see my team's

> "You miss 100% of the shots you don't take."
>
> *Wayne Gretzky*

focus shift. They started to work closer together and started supporting one another. They also started following all of the "show time" behaviors that were in the materials. We started to get busier because our guests were happy, which meant the client was making more money. Everyone was winning!

The second part of my plan had to do with the guests. Everything I had read pointed to creating a strong emotional connection with guests. We needed that. I really don't think the guests felt that they had a say in what we did, and we needed to change that. So, I posted signs all over campus requesting that guests come to our cafe after we closed on Wednesday. Chef David and I would be there to hear them out. We were interested in what they liked; but more than that, we were really interested in where they thought we could improve upon and how we could create a great experience for them and their co-workers.

To my delight, on Wednesday afternoon after a long day of work, there was a long line of guests waiting to come in and give us that valuable feedback. I remember grabbing David and saying, "Look, Chef, this is so awesome! The guests are showing up, and they have so much to tell us!" Chef David did not see it the way I did. He seemed surprised and annoyed as if he did not expect anyone to come. He shook his head, grabbed his jacket, and walked out the back door. I didn't care. I was super excited and ready to listen. I set up my table and opened the doors.

The guests might as well have had torches and pitchforks. My meeting with them was brutal. They beat me up for at least an hour (it felt like several hours) with 135 changes they felt we needed to make. I took all of their concerns seriously and started making changes. Most importantly, I began creating personal relationships with the guests.

The crazy thing was that we actually started to make money. As corporate began to see the reports of our progress, they were anxious to know what was going on. They sent auditors three times to inspect and evaluate our performance. Each time, we were better than the time before. If you recall, we were on the verge of losing the contract. But once the changes were implemented and the results were reviewed, our client removed the closure notice and awarded us a 10-year contract. But an even greater reward was when the CEO and CFO came out to see what we were doing and designated our operation as a "Center for Excellence (CFE)," the highest distinction for a select few accounts in our company, the best of the best. The worst thing that had ever happened became the best thing that had ever happened!

Much of the credit goes to Chef David who pushed me from theory to application. The words on the scattered pages across my desk of all the things I had learned came alive in the life of our work and made all the difference.

As a result of my success, I started getting promoted. Other companies, managers, and chefs visited to see what we were doing.

This momentum was pushing us higher and farther than we ever dreamed.

Never despise your adversity. I had never failed before this massive error, so I got caught in a downward spiral. It took this obstacle to squeeze greatness out of me. Who knows where I would have been if this failure had not occurred? As a result, my career really took off.

Eurest Dining Services (now Eurest) was a growing company in the foodservice business and industry sector, and under the dynamic leadership of Rick Post, we really hit our stride. Our clients were very diverse and included those from manufacturing plants to the most innovative technical companies in the world. Eurest was really the only home-grown sector in the Compass Group family. All of the other operating sectors were acquisitions with existing visions, values and their own operating cultures. Eurest was new, and as it was growing, it needed structure, defining pillars, and a purpose. As the company defined itself, it would need a culture focused on its guests, both internal and external. I believe everything happens for a reason and it was no mistake that I ended up here. I was so lucky and clearly I was in the right place.

A year after being designated a Center for Excellence, I was promoted to District Manager. I loved that role managing a fine group of managers, and supporting a diverse variety of clients was truly awesome. Two years later, I was offered a position as the Director of CFEs for all of Eurest. This was my first above-unit support role, and I loved the idea of working with the best operators in the business. Another advantage to this role is that it brought me closer to leadership. I reported directly to the CEO and helped our Division Presidents with challenges in the field. I was able to share my ideas around hospitality and demonstrate how a people-first approach could solve a lot of challenges. We had a lot of success, including great retention numbers, as well as three years of tremendous growth. Leadership fully endorsed my approach, and as a result, they created a role for me. I became the Vice President of Guest Experience, truly my dream job! Making sure that both our external and internal guests are heard and attended to, my team now spends half of its time training, onboarding, and inspiring our operational teams, and the other half studying and interacting with guests and clients.

What did I learn? Don't reject your failures. Learn from them. I realized that setbacks were really just a part of the process on the road to excellence.

Chapter 4
Choosing the Right People

Early in my career as a manager, I was looking for a grill cook. The labor market was tough, and this was an open kitchen where the person in the position of grill cook had direct interaction with our guests. I had gotten some interest, but was not getting any qualified applicants. One morning, a young man named Damon applied. He came for an interview and I really liked him. The challenge was that he had *no* cooking experience. So, I asked Chef David to take Damon to the kitchen to see what he could do. It didn't go well. He truly had no culinary skills or knowledge. But we were desperate, and we both liked Damon. We took a calculated risk and decided to give this inexperienced candidate a chance. That is when the magic started.

Though Damon had no experience, he had a strong mind and was incredibly likeable. Almost immediately, he acquired the skills needed

> "Hospitality is almost impossible to teach. It's all about hiring the right people."
>
> *Danny Meyer*

to become a solid grill cook. But then he began to soar. In the seven years prior to Damon coming to work for me, we made about $700 a day during the breakfast daypart. Just 30 days after I hired Damon, sales rose to more than $1,000 a day for that same daypart. By day 90, we hit an all-time sales high of $1,500 a day at breakfast. I wondered, "What happened?" The answer was simple: Damon happened.

Damon was nice, thoughtful, and the guests really liked him. They liked him so much that they told other people about him. Those people came to visit, fell in love with Damon, and became loyal guests.

Damon worked for me for seven years, and I promoted him four times. His impact on my leadership style was profound. Because of what I saw happen with him, I shifted my personnel philosophy. I started hiring for attitude versus skill. I realized that I can teach a person to run a register or make a pizza. Almost anyone can learn that. It is much more difficult to teach the mindset that creates stellar hospitality. It was something that Damon did naturally.

A few years into working together, Damon and I were chatting, and he made a bold confession. The day I met him was his third day in the United States, and the job I offered him was the first job he ever had. His skill set may have shown this, but definitely not his attitude. This success story shows the benefits of hiring for a great attitude and a willingness to learn because they can far outweigh learned skills.

Finding the Right People

So, what is the process for choosing the right people? Let's start with where to look. Now more than ever, there are many great avenues for seeking out new team members:

- Indeed
- Glassdoor
- Google Jobs
- Craigslist
- Monster
- CareerBuilder
- LinkedIn

All of these options are modern and user-friendly. You can even ask screening questions on many of them and determine which resumes you want to see based on the answers of the candidates. It's a great time-saver. I'm a huge advocate for posting job openings in non-traditional places like churches and schools. I have found some of my best applicants this way.

Crafting the Right Posting

Next comes crafting your job posting. Regardless of platform, many of the job postings I see are far too generic. In many cases, I don't believe they are even asking for the skills they are really looking for in a candidate. So it's no wonder they don't end up with a pool of qualified candidates from which they can draw. For example, one posting read: "Local law firm looking for receptionist; skills required include organization, communication, and computer skills."

Really? This is going to attract the very people the company does not want because it will merely attract job seekers. These will be people who work just enough so they don't get fired. They will not add anything special or valuable to the guest experience. Instead, they might have better luck finding what they're looking for if they posted the following: "Local law firm seeking an ambassador of first impressions. Skills required include the ability to make every guest that enters our office feel that they are special and that they have come to the right place."

This the language that will spark the attention of a real go-getter. So, lead with what you need. You can check for the other skill sets during the interview process. And if they are fabulous enough, you might be willing to invest in training them in skills that are missing just to have that sparkling personality as the face of your company at the reception desk, just as I did when hiring Damon.

I always incorporate words like smiling, team, high energy, and thoughtful when posting a job. A mentor of mine once used the fishing analogy that I always come back to: "Use the right bait to attract what you are looking for."

A person with great hospitality skills has certain qualities. Most importantly, they are always smiling and tend to bring the best version of themselves to the interview. The exhaustive list of qualities is quite long, but a short sampling would include traits like:

- Openness
- Natural friendliness
- A good listener
- Calmness
- Creativity
- Flexibility

Conducting the Right Interview

The interview is really the casting call for the star performer. It is all about casting the best performer for the role. Think of yourself as a multi-million dollar casting agent. You know the type of person the director needs. Now you have to find them. You would not hire the goofiness and likability of Jim Carrey for a role that needs the seriousness and depth of Morgan Freeman. Make sure you know what you are looking for when you sit down with the interviewee.

The interview is the strongest tool in selecting the best person. Though you may be tempted to skip over them, it's important that you ask the basic (and quite frankly boring) interview questions:

- Tell me about yourself.
- Why do you want this job?
- What strengths and weaknesses do you bring to the organization?

- What attracted you to this company?

These are questions all managers ask when hiring, which is exactly the problem. The candidate has practiced their answers so many times, they almost sound robotic. A better tactic is to follow these common questions with ones that really drill down to the heart of the person and test their honesty, skills with people, ability to think on their feet, and reveal their true personality and attitude.

- Tell me about a co-worker who was impossible to work with and how you dealt with them.
- Tell me about something that has happened in your career that you hope never happens again.
- What was your best day at work, one that was unforgettable?
- If I gave you $100,000 to start a business, what type of business would you start?
- Tell me a time at work when you made a really big mistake.

But my favorite, and the one I think is the best interview question of them all, is:

- How many questions did you prepare to ask me today?

The last question is a great question because it tells you if your company was just one among a list of companies they applied to, or if the person had done any research into your company and has come prepared to learn about it. Or perhaps they are just looking for a job, and any job will do. If the latter is the case, you may still consider hiring them. But I wouldn't do it without a second interview where I asked the same question.

Improve your interview experience by using new technology like Hirevue, which offers pre-employment testing and online interviewing software. You might use this service to pre-screen candidates so that only the best of the best get invited in for a face-to-face interview. Whether online or in-person, interaction is always the best way to gauge an applicant's natural demeanor.

Top Tips for Interviewers

After interviewing my share of applicants, whether for positions I was hiring for or when assisting other colleagues, I've learned a few tips along the way. Keep in mind that the candidate should do 80% of talking while you do 20%.

- Don't jump right in, but help the candidate relax. Start with a question, even if it is an easy one, rather starting by telling them about yourself or the company. Keeping the candidate slightly on edge is a great way to test his or her temperament.
- Make the time to do it right. If you do not have the time to do it right, where will you find the time to do it again?

- Know the job and the format you will use to control the interview. Use pre-scripted open-ended questions to obtain the greatest knowledge of the applicant in the shortest time period.
- Be an effective communicator, and more importantly, a good listener.
- Make certain the applicant feels comfortable and at ease. A relaxed candidate will give you a better interview, will divulge more information, and will provide a better understanding of how they might function within your team. Once the interview is well underway, you should interject comments or even humor to ease the tension.
- Pay attention to body language and style of dress. Both are good indicators about who the person is. Listen for well-thought out responses and the verbiage used in those responses.
- Collect background information as early as possible, perhaps in the pre-interview so you can screen out any potential problems. Verify and check for experience level, stability, and performance, gaps in employment, organization, and self-insight.
- Look for personality and strong interpersonal skills. Do they smile? Do they laugh at a joke or sit there stone-faced?
- Check for traits, such as pride, energy, enthusiasm, attitude, communicative nature, and team orientation. The majority of

time spent interviewing should be focused on the personality of the interviewee rather than their experience or skills.
- Using consistent questions and utilizing an interview scorecard helps you more easily measure the responses of each applicant.

Two Master-Level Tips

Often during an interview, there are times of silence. Both interviewers and interviewees feel uncomfortable when there is silence in a one-on-one conversation, but silence is ok. Pause between the candidate's response and before asking the next question. This will sometimes compel the candidate to continue talking where you will learn information about them that you would not normally have learned. Remember, the candidate should be talking the majority of the time.

Next, allow other members of your team to interview the final candidates. The involvement of the team sends a clear message to both parties that this is a team atmosphere and decision. Getting your team involved will ensure that you hire the right applicant and that they will take an active role in the new hire's success. Your team will not hesitate to tell you why they think the person is or is not right for the team. In fact, I believe that the higher the position, the more eyes you should have on each candidate. We have all seen what happens when teams or groups hire within their own vacuum. The worst thing you can do as a leader is to hire solely with your gut, make a mistake, and put the wrong person in the wrong position. Use all of the resources at your disposal and don't take the hiring decision lightly.

As a leader, you create the culture. When team members feel as if they are important, critical, and valuable, they want to rise to meet the challenges you set before them. They need to know that you care. It draws on that common theme we've explored a few times so far: emotion. Caring is like a mirror. When you show people that you care, they reflect that care back to you and then out to your clientele. Many managers undervalue the power of this to their own peril. They think that strong-arming and intimidating their employees is the right strategy. Other managers want to create a culture where there is symbiosis between managers and employees. They simply don't know how to create it. Now, you know.

Chapter 5

Investing in the Right People

Emerging technology, new business models, and changing guest demographics are forcing companies to rethink the way they hire. There was a time when skill sets were the key to getting a job. Then, it shifted to education. For a brief time, it revolved around experience. Today, though, more and more companies understand that they must hire for attitude and train for behavior. They know that if you have the right attitude, you can learn anything.

> "Synergy – the bonus that is achieved when things work together harmoniously."
>
> Mark Twain

Getting your strategy right means aligning the business' values and putting the right people in the right places to execute the vision. Business is people as much as it is technology, product, or service. It is paramount to have people in whom you can invest the time and training to develop them into superstars.

That training is a powerful element. You need to go one step further beyond having the right people in the right places; you must also ensure that they know what to do once they get there. And if you have screened for the people with the right mindset, the process of knowledge acquisition is easy.

Big picture thinking means understanding how your teams need to work within the company and how to interface with guests, clients, and partners to deliver maximum value. Therefore, creating a world-class team starts with selecting the right candidates. This is not a step that can be skipped. If you hire the wrong people, all of the fancy management techniques won't bail you out. Low-cost employees are not low cost if they quit after three months because the cost to replace them and train that replacement will far exceed what you were paying for the poor employee. You can teach people to run the register, but you can't teach them to be nice.

Onboarding

A new associate is never more focused, malleable, and teachable than on their first day on the job. Most companies choose Day 1 to fill out all of the paperwork and read the employee handbook. Avoid the temptation of the "Day 1 Data Dump." The last thing a new hire wants to do on Day 1 is fill out forms. Instead, a proper onboarding is about making introductions. Introduce the new hire to the team, walk through the workflow, and acclimate them to their new work environment.

Your onboarding strategy should have both structure and uniformity. Demographic changes to the workforce have changed expectations. Millennials and Generation Z will expect a structured onboarding. They do not function well in an environment where onboarding is off the cuff or an afterthought. Some key pieces to onboarding:

- Send something to the new hire's home prior to starting (a simple handwritten note works). It speaks volumes about the team culture.
- Make plenty of time for proper introductions.
- Provide a detailed site tour.
- Take the time to walk them through the vision and values, both within your team and those of the company.
- Regardless of position, have them work their first few days with your best team member, even if their jobs are not related. You want the best of the best transferring their positivity to the new hire.
- As the hiring manager, stay close. Within 30 days, conduct a "Stay Interview" where you solidify them as a part of the team and address any concerns they may have. Stay interviews help managers understand why employees stay and what might cause them to leave.

- Onboarding must go past the first 30 days. The structure should include a workbook outline and frequent check-ins. This type of investment goes a long way in ensuring that the associate doesn't leave.

My team spends a lot of our time looking for hospitality-minded people. The selection process can be long. But in the end, we know that when we cast the right person into the right role and we onboard them correctly, they will reward our guests and their co-workers, and will be satisfied in their job.

The Guest Whisperer

Throughout my career, I searched for ways to interact with our guests. I sought out every possible opportunity for talking with them and listening to what they had to say. Many times when we faced challenges in the field, I would suggest facilitating focus groups with our guests. This process caught fire! Clients loved the idea of giving guests a voice, guests really enjoyed providing feedback and seeing their suggestions come to life, and operators saw the benefits of increased sales and guest loyalty that came from the process. We created a six sigma proprietary process that became a tremendous success.

As of today, I have personally met with over 150,000 guests in a variety of business types, and it has changed me. I now see the business from the guest's viewpoint and am able to articulate that vision to our creative team. Our Marketing and Culinary teams utilize the data we collect to create spaces and offerings that resonate with our guests because they were built directly as a result of their feedback.

Through this, I learned quickly that one size does not fit all. Business type, geography, demographic, and gender each had a huge influence on the food we served, the marketing we featured, and the service we delivered. Lunch at a manufacturing site in Seattle is much different than lunch at a large insurance company in Boston. This became a huge competitive advantage for us! I think to this day, no one has spoken directly to more guests than I have, and it has become a piece of professional pride for me. Through frontline trainings, I've also spoken with more internal team members than most, which has shaped so much of what we do.

As time progressed, we added technology solutions to our Voice of the Customer platform because we wanted to make it easier for guests to interact with us. It was around this time that the millennial generation hit the workforce and became our guests and our team members. The great news was that we were not caught by surprise. We had been listening to them as they matured and we understood them. This generation was a game changer; a keystone generation that would have a long term effect on all of us.

According to Pew Research, millennials are typically referred to as people who were born between 1981 and 1996. Some interesting facts they shared about the millennial generation include:

- They earn, on average, $10,000 less than their parents did at the same age.
- They are typically drowning in student loan debt.
- A third of them still live at home with their parents.
- They are the largest working class in the marketplace.
- They are the most generous of all generations when it comes to charitable giving.
- They are more concerned about the environment than any other issue.

This is great information, but it doesn't necessarily give us a good understanding of them. From talking with them, we personally have learned that the millennial generation:

- Loves to communicate through technology
- Are motivated by sustainability
- Hold wellness as a high priority
- Are great multitaskers and collaborators
- Have all of the skills needed to contribute to a highly effective team.

As a company, we are incredibly successful because we understand our guests. The added bonus is that many of our guests and our team members are the same age and are seeking the same things. So in addition to creating great environments for our millennial guests, we also created training, onboarding, and programs that would drive loyalty for our millennial team members.

A few years back, we started to hear about Gen Z, and that this generation would have as comparable of an impact on the workplace as millennials. In order to get ahead of this, I started visiting colleges and having focus groups with students and faculty. I really enjoyed my time with Gen Zers. They are practical, positive, and focused. PEW Research states the following:

- This group surpasses all preceding generations as the most ethically, racially, educationally, and socio-economically diverse.
- 25% of American Generation Z are Hispanic.
- They love the planet and want to protect it.
- They are passionate about their diverse positions on social issues.

These are broad and sweeping generalizations, for sure. But the trends have been proven to hold in study after study. Since many of your team members and leaders will fall into this category, you should know what drives them.

Coaches versus Leaders

Younger generations are motivated by leaders who coach them. They want a leader who respects their skills, understands their inexperience, and cares about them professionally. This generation is looking for you to create a clear vision and help them figure out how they can move their career forward. They are style-specific and are looking for coaches and collaborators.

As a leader, take advantage of the great skills these generations offer. They are great multi-taskers, so you need to constantly challenge them with new tasks. They are great researchers, so challenge them to find answers. They are out of the box thinkers, so don't lock them in to a single solution. In fact, encourage unorthodox solutions.

Collaboration versus Competition

In my early days leading teams, I would create competitions pitting one team member against another to create solutions. That won't work with the younger generations today. In general, they prefer to work together and to seek solutions as a group. This is a great quality! It promotes a much tighter knit team and removes all of the negative politicking that can occur with competition.

Flexible Work Environments vs. Fixed Work Hours

The 9-5 workday has disappeared, especially in retail. There is tremendous value in empowering your team to hit realistic deadlines and not dictating when they do it. This approach provides the freedom that will motivate younger generations and generate loyalty to you and the company. Be flexible and hold them accountable.

Reward and Recognition

This generation truly enjoys recognition. It's a gift to them. Celebrating success is something most companies don't do well. Be sure there is a clear system for recognition in place, and allow team members to recognize one another (they love this!). Use recognition to motivate performance, and most importantly, reinforce company values. Recognition for innovation is my personal favorite as it reminds the team that we are always looking for what is next.

Training for Purpose

As you build your team with all ages, genders, races, and ethnicities, they will need to train to acquire the skills that will empower them to perform on a stellar level. The best gift a workplace can give to a team member is purpose. Once you hire the right people, it's critical to align them with your purpose. Great leaders create clear direction, then empower their teams to personalize and execute on that direction. Driving hospitality and providing great guest experiences is hard work and seldom happens by mistake. In the next section we will discuss how to inspire teams to provide world-class service.

Our Secret Weapon

The millennial generation is a keystone generation, instead of adopting practices from the prior generation, Generation X, the millennials have blazed their own trail. Perhaps the biggest area of transformation is around communication. From social media to texting and Zoom meetings, the millennials have changed the way we communicate. You can see Boomers and Xers are following the millennials just by looking at the current state of Facebook where you'll find grandmothers and teenagers interacting and sharing photos with their Facebook community. Opportunity was knocking. We had a generation that we felt would fundamentally change the workplace and real world examples made it clear to us the other generations would follow. I just kept thinking that this would be a time to revolutionize how we communicate with the frontline in a way that enhances productivity, drives team loyalty and enriches the entire organization. Our search was on.

As a team, we were searching feverishly for an application that could be used across the workplace. My team member Alison Lambert and I held weekly meetings with outside companies looking for a game changer, an established company or a startup that saw what we were seeing. We felt the improvements in personal, yet virtual, communication could be applied in the workplace and that we could create a sense of community, making our really big company feel really small, and most importantly, connected.

The process was frustrating. We saw some cool applications, but no company put what we were looking for in a simple, clean format. The companies we spoke to seemed to be very inflexible with their products, not to mention their capabilities. We wanted a solution that was high touch that we could personalize but we kept seeing total automation. We started toying with creating something ourselves when word of something really cool came our way from the great white north.

Our Canadian technology team, Compass Digital Labs, held a contest with several small startup companies. The idea was simple and brilliant: allow the companies to present their innovations and the winning startup would win a contract and trial opportunity with Compass Group Canada. Nudge, an employee engagement app, was the winner. The Nudge app creates a communication chain throughout all levels of an organization, from headquarters to the frontline. For the sake of comparison, imagine Facebook for work.

Nudge was founded on the guiding philosophy that today's workforce expects a seamless, familiar experience, and was purposely designed to empower frontline team members with the tools, knowledge, and support to be inspired to do great work every day. After spending the last decade studying high-performing teams – how they work, what they need, what they like – Nudge applied these insights to design a platform that enables frontline teams to deliver an exceptional guest experience, every day.

Delivering directly to the frontline via push notifications with gamification to inspire and connect the workforce, Nudge inspires teams and team members to do great work every day. Alison and I recognized that this platform was exactly what we were looking for. We couldn't wait to meet with the company and run a trial in our business.

That's when we found the second, yet most important, ingredient of the Nudge platform – the people behind it! When we met Jordan Ekers, Jess Skillings, and Julia Mignelli, we were impressed with their product knowledge, but more importantly, we immediately hit it off because they we so like-minded. They listened to us and our needs and went far out of their way to understand our business and what we were looking to accomplish. In Nudge we found a company that was eager to share knowledge and to collaborate with us. We learned from each other and have celebrated some incredible success.

We are able to message and have two-way communication with the frontline every day with an open rate of around 80%. Think about that for a moment – 80%! Most internal corporate memos from executives are lucky to hit a 40% open rate. Keep in mind that this is a voluntary app and our frontline opens and acts on the Nudges they receive at an

80% clip. We just expanded our reach exponentially and engaged a frontline that was eager to act. This has been game changing!

We are messaging our frontline important cultural, training, safety, and personal development content every day. Not only are they listening, but they are sharing their needs, wants, and best practices back with us and with one another. The two-way communication became such a powerful tool for us. We ask the field questions and receive thousands of responses from all levels of the organization. The effect has been twofold: we surfaced powerful solutions to challenges directly from the teams that provide service to our guests every day, which in turn translated to an unprecedented level of team engagement across our organization. We have been able to tap into the collective wisdom of our frontline, and empower them with a voice to guide our company's operational direction. Further, in real-time, we are able to uncover the drivers of team satisfaction simply by opening a two-way communication channel, and the impact on our culture has been resoundingly positive. We experienced an immediate improvement in productivity, a reduction in team turnover, and we were able to capture incredibly rich and new insights from our field to guide our guest and our overall team experience.

My teammate Alison Lambert powers the Nudge engine for our company, and I want to recognize her. We have a thriving, connected community, and I see fantastic results in our future.

Our partnership with Nudge isn't solely based on their great product, though. From the beginning, they connected with us on an emotional level; they listened to us and led with a hospitality mindset. That was their edge.

Chapter 6
"Show Time" Behaviors

Zingerman's is an iconic gourmet food market in Ann Arbor, Michigan. Known widely for their food, their deep-rooted hospitality exceeds even their finest offerings. On one of my professional visits to the market, I caught them at the end of their daily huddle. The manager was standing in the doorway between the back of the house and the front of the house. The message he was delivering to his team was simple and perfect.

> "Instead of focusing on the competition, focus on the customer."
>
> Scott Cook

"Team, when you cross this threshold to the front of the house, our guests are present. It's SHOW TIME, and you're on!"

What an amazing motivational mantra to give the team as they start their day of providing exceptional service to their guests. Let's dig in to what was meant when he said, "It's SHOW TIME!" It's clear that he was setting an expectation about the behaviors he wanted to see from the team, a standard established by a true leader. It is the high bar he asks the team to jump. But that expectation also inherently expresses a vote of confidence that each team member will use his or her unique personality, skills, and methods to put on the best show possible. Setting the bar high for the team must also leave room for your team to personalize each experience for your guests. Hospitality is at its best when it's authentic, and your team is at their best when they feel free to be authentically who they are! Give your team the flexibility to show who they are, thereby allowing them to connect directly with their guests. The following are the bare minimum "show time" behaviors that I expect from my team.

Smile

The most basic of the "show time" behaviors is also the most powerful gesture that can be extended from one human to another. Before there was spoken language, humans communicated with body language. The smile told strangers a lot about a person in those primitive days, most importantly, that there was no ill will intended. Imagine

> "A smile is the universal welcome!"
>
> Max Eastman

how frightening it must have been to happen upon a stranger in primitive times. Meeting a stranger could mean the start of a new alliance or it could mean certain death. But a simple smile indicated safety and hospitality. A smile conveys all of the right things to another person. It says I am friendly, welcoming, and willing to help you. It instantly fills you up. It's why when you walk down the street and smile at a total stranger, they smile back. Babies practice their first smiles soon after birth and have the skill practically mastered between six and 12 weeks of age. Smiling lowers the heart rates and blood pressures of both the person smiling and the person who is being smiled at, according to a study done by the University of London. In fact, the same study showed that people who were smiled regularly had a 35% chance of living longer than sour pusses. Other studies show that a propensity to smile was associated with higher levels of financial success. How's that for an incentive to flash those pearly whites? But in hospitality, the smile is the golden calling card. It's "show time," and a smile is how we start. If you get anything from this, it's that a smile is one of the most powerful things you can do from one person to another.

Eye Contact

In a Business Insider article, A. J. Harbinger, author of "The Art of Charm", writes, "Eye contact is one of the easiest and most powerful ways to make a person feel recognized, understood, and validated. The simple act of holding someone's gaze — whether it's a new girl, a prospective employer, or an old friend — has the power to ignite or deepen a relationship." When you look someone in the eye, it establishes trust. Eye contact and acknowledgement lets guests know you see them and eliminates apprehension and stress. It makes the list of basic "show time" behaviors because guests need to know that you are laser-focused on their needs. When you make eye contact, it should be deep and intense without looking away. It establishes a strong and immediate connection.

Greetings

Greetings are perhaps the most underrated aspects of hospitality. Part of that might stem from all the yelling going on in fast-casual restaurants. Greetings need to be unique and sincere. When you walk into a store and all the employees scream, "Welcome to wherever!" you are unimpressed because it is just so insincere and impersonal. For starters, the employees barely look up, except to notice that the doors have opened. And they all sound like robots repeating a line that they have been coached to say. It is clear that they are not greeting from a genuine desire to welcome you. Rather, the supervisor is watching and will punish them if they fail to say the magic words. But those rote, mechanical greetings have no magic in them. The magic is in the heart and spirit of the greeter. Greetings are a great way to start interactions and can set the tone of a visit. With regulars, hearing the words, "Welcome back!" ignites their loyalty. Remembering their names is a major bonus that can create a guest for life. For new guests, asking

"Hi, how are you?" is a powerful greeting because it invokes a response, letting the guest know you actually want to hear from them. The greeting integrates with the first two "show time" behaviors—smiling and making eye contact—into a show stopping way to make a powerful first impression.

Appearance

Guests judge everything about us by how we look and how we behave. Unfortunately it doesn't matter whether or not you think that's fair. It's true, so we have to be prepared for that. In fact, we can use it to our advantage. When we look sharp, we are more apt to approach others with confidence. When we add a clean and polished appearance to a smile, eye contact, and a strong greeting, the interaction is sure to get off to a great start. I am also very happy to see the slow elimination of standard uniforms in both restaurants and retail. Giving our teams flexibility to personalize their look is trendy and interesting for guests to look at. Allowing team members' personality and individuality come through on the floor will enhance the experience for guests. It goes without saying, but be sure your dress standards match the brand identity and are appropriate for your business.

Expressing oneself brings me to tattoos, piercings, and overall appearances, which takes me back to Portland, Oregon, where I conducted an orientation training for a large group. I remember taking the stage, looking out, and thinking, "This is the happiest tattooed and pierced group I have ever seen!" They were wonderful! I understand that you must make decisions based on your environment, but I also feel that body art should not be a judge of character, but instead a means for showing personality and passion. Many studies have shown that individuals who have the creative gene lean toward visual displays that include creative dress, tattoos, and piercings.

Be Present

"Show time" behaviors start with you being present with guests. Make every interaction count from how you answer a simple question to more complicated interactions. The team needs to practice *guest focus*. Many of us have had the experience of being in a store surrounded by team members focused on tasks. They may be restocking, cleaning, or talking to each other while not intentionally ignoring guests. But to the guest, every second that they are ignored is equivalent to a minute. Time moves differently for your guest than it does for your team. The team member might think, "Let me just take five seconds to put the last three bottles of cream on the shelf," but to the guest, the message is, "You are not my priority and I don't value your time." Your culture will separate task and purpose so that the team understands that their purpose is to delight guests, which always takes precedence over a task. Being present is like being with your best friend—your full and undivided attention is the gift you give them.

Fond Farewells

Just as greetings are critical, farewells are a major part of the "show time" experience. It is your last in-person opportunity to impress your signature brand of hospitality on your guests. Thanking them and inviting them to come back is critical. Walt Disney felt that guests remember what happens last the most. He called it Peak End Theory. It's the reason that every day at Disney parks end with a parade and fireworks. It is not an accident. Similarly in the hotel industry, several retail studies show that guests rate their experience based on their interaction at checkout.

I can personally attest to the fact that the Peak End Theory is in fact effective. It was mid-August a few years ago that I got a call from my sister in Massachusetts. She wanted to bring her family to visit me in Florida and go to Walt Disney World. I tried to talk her out of coming to Florida in the summer, but she was set on the idea. Surely enough, 10 days later, my sister, her husband, and their two boys were at my house and we were headed to Disney.

After only 10 minutes of being at the park, I could tell that this was going to be the worst day ever! As soon as we enter the park, my sister and her husband start arguing, the boys were crying, and I was looking for the nearest beer garden. It was only 9 a.m.! And since we were at Disney, I knew we'd be there for the whole, painful day.

I wish I could tell you that things got better, that our day improved, but it didn't. I will never forget when I saw that first firework go off. I turned to my wife and said, "Thank God! We are out of here!" It was the happiest I had seen her all day.

At the time, the fireworks were a precursor for the parade. We found a great spot and waited for the cast of characters to pass by. About mid-parade my nephew Joey saw his favorite character and ran out and hugged him. It was a truly magic moment! I turned to my left to see my sister's reaction. She had tears of joy running down her face, and she looked me in the eye and exclaimed, "This was the best day ever!" I can assure you that it most certainly wasn't, but it didn't matter because nothing else that we experienced that day mattered. This moment at the end of the day was all my sister and her family would remember.

Peak End Theory is real. I have used this story in guest experience training over the years. Even though it was a hot, miserable time at the park, those joyful moments at the end of the day locked in a positive overall experience.

The Daily Huddle

Communication and training need to be a daily event. It's critical for the team to get together and have a pre-shift meeting every day. Daily huddles should be interactive and cover a variety of topics. As a frontline manager, my team typically reviewed the following topics:

- New product introductions
- Store specials

- Safety topics
- Special events, birthdays, and anniversaries
- Recap from the day prior
- Goal setting: let's be faster/friendlier/sell more
- Manager-led recognition and team rewards

We always closed with team kudos, allowing team members to acknowledge one another. This is a great bonding event where team members get to tell others about amazing "show time" behaviors they witnessed from their peers that perhaps the manager did not see. Your meetings should have structure so that they are brief. But they should also bring the energy to set the tone for every shift. Don't compromise or settle; have team huddles every day without exception.

Chapter 7

Service Recovery

In every business, things will go wrong. How you react to those challenges will define your brand and your culture. More than that, it will set you apart from the competition and help you retain your client base. Author Jeffery Gitomer said it best:

"It's not the apology that matters; it's the recovery that counts!"

The Front Door vs. The Back Door

Companies spend millions to acquire new customers. But their efforts are thwarted when they don't pay enough attention to the exit of their existing customer due to service issues that could have been easily solved. Companies can expect to invest nearly five times more to lure a new customer than it costs to retain an existing one.

There are many ways to calculate the cost of losing a guest. Many companies use these calculations to help put the value of each customer in perspective. In the highly competitive pizza delivery market, they calculate the loss of one family is worth $10,000 a year.

Losing even a single customer is a multi-faceted pounding to the company's bottom line.

Let's assume that you run a bed-and-breakfast in a resort town. You have just 20 rooms available for guests to rent throughout the year. Now imagine that Peter and Kate Bachman come to visit every year with their three sons, their wives, and children, an event which they have named "The Bachman Beach Bash." If Peter and Kate have a negative experience, they may choose not to return next year. At $210 per night for the five nights of their yearly vacation, you may calculate that the loss is equal to $210 times five, or $1,050. Multiply that loss over the number of years Peter and Kate were likely to return, and the losses start to become quite significant.

In addition to the loss of the Bachman's present and future business, there is also value to loss of any marketing that they see for the bed-and-breakfast. While marketing materials may pique the interest of someone who has never been to your establishment, any advertising seen by Peter and Kate will be a reminder of the poor experience they had and will reignite their negative feelings toward your bed-and-breakfast. Now that Peter and Kate are no longer patronizing your establishment, you can be sure that their family members have heard about the experience and are looking elsewhere for accommodations for the upcoming season. Furthermore, Peter and Kate serve as negative advertisement for the business and their family members serve as distanced negative advertisements. So even though

Peter's son did not have a bad experience, he will piggyback on the bad experience of his parents in telling people that they should not book there. It is nearly impossible to put a dollar value on this negative feedback loop. Think back to the last really bad experience you had as a client or guest. Feel that? It still has the ability to get your blood boiling.

One of the newer and more hard-hitting ways customers ensure that their voices are heard is by posting on social media sites like Facebook, Google, and Yelp. If riots are the language of the unheard, social media is the riot of the unheard customer. Some customers will spend precious time posting on every site they can think of so that they can let others know to stay away. The good news (if you want to call it that) is that the majority of dissatisfied customers simply leave and never return without making any effort to tell others to beware. According to White House office of Consumer Affairs, dissatisfied customers typically tell nine to 15 other people about their experience, while approximately 13% tell upwards of 20 people.

All told, the price tag for losing Peter and Kate could be in the tens of thousands. It would not be exaggerating to say that most estimates are conservative. So why take the chance if it is possible to recover a customer that is slipping away?

There is one overarching question to the issue of the angry customer: why are they really upset? The "why" question is one that many companies skirt over too quickly. When the manager gets called in to deal with an irate customer, they are usually addressing the "what" of the situation. What happened? What was said? What was done? What can I do to make this go away? Of course, you have to know the facts about what happened. But it is more important for you and your teams to understand why guests are upset and how to put in place an awesome recovery plan.

> "Your most unhappy customers are your greatest source of learning."
>
> Bill Gates

Perhaps it will help to think of it this way: When military forces go out on missions, their goal is to bring back all of men and women involved in the mission. In fact, the U. S. Army Rangers have as one of its mottos: "Never leave a man behind; I will never leave a fallen comrade to fall into the hands of the enemy." But missions fail (just like hospitality service plans). When a mission fails and a soldier is caught and captured, a massive recovery effort is put in place to get that soldier back. Even one soldier left behind is deemed wholly unacceptable. So the recovery team goes in stealthily and carefully to extract that soldier and return him or her to the squad.

The same mindset needs to be applied to your business (though the stakes are not as high). You never want to leave a customer behind if there is any chance of saving the relationship.

Complaints occur when there is a gap between the service that is expected and the service that is delivered. 1Financial Training Services cites that while 96% of unhappy customers don't complain, 91% of those will never return. So when you do get a complaint, consider it a gift. The first step to an awesome recovery is understanding that.

Service recovery, when done correctly, is that unique opportunity to take an unhappy guest and transform them so that you not only retain them as a loyal customer, but you also create an advocate for your business, all in one brilliantly crafted and strategic move. Statistically, about 68% of customers who stop doing business with an organization do so because of perceived indifference on the part of the employees (Bloomtools).

What does perceived indifference look like? Below are some of the phrases and body language signals that indicate to the guest that your company really does not care. Some are slight; others are extreme. But they all lend to the belief that a guests' dollars are just not that important to you:

- Failing to say, "Thank you," especially with sincerity
- Forgetting a regular customer's name or face
- Failing to deliver on stated or printed promises
- Shrugging shoulders

- Saying things like, "I'm sorry, sir, there is nothing I can do."
- Referring repeatedly to company policy in the middle of conflict with a guest
- Failing to tell a guest about upcoming specials, promotions, or sales
- Not taking responsibility for mistakes
- Refusing to engage in conversation
- Telling a customer that you are not authorized to address their problem
- Letting phones ring incessantly without answering (that sends a message to both the in-person customer and the customer on the phone)
- Making customers wait without acknowledging them
- Failing to return phone calls
- Leaving customers on hold for long periods of time (Hint: 30 seconds is a long time)
- Failing to tell customers that you want them to do business with you again

Whew, it's a long list! And it is by no means exhaustive. These are just the blatant ways in which companies unintentionally open the back door and send guests away instead of opening the front door and showing that the guest is valued. This is why your entire team must be trained and empowered to perform service recovery.

The Definitive Guide to Service Recovery

Service recovery really is quite simple if you have the end game firmly in mind. You want to covert an angry customer into a strong brand advocate. To do so, I recommend using the **PLEASE** response method. Whenever I have been approached with a guest challenge this has worked for me:

Prepare

Prepare yourself to hear an angry rant. Guests often get themselves worked up over a perceived slight and may say some things that they should not say. Unhappy guests can be challenging. You need to be in the right frame of mind to create a solution. Maintain your composure, decorum, and politeness. When the interaction ends positively, you will be delighted.

Of course, the most effective strategy for dealing with a complaint is to ensure that there is no need to lodge a complaint in the first place. Learning to anticipate guests' needs and going above and beyond their expectations as a matter of regular operating philosophy will help to eliminate many of the complaints that happen on a regular basis.

Actively Listen

Don't interrupt a guest who is ranting. They are letting off the steam. You must allow them to exhaust their concerns. Let them get from the beginning of their complaint to the end. When they conclude, do not respond by offering excuses or trying to explain away aspects of the failure.

When a guest comes to you with a complaint, you must own it immediately without forcing the guest to convince you that there is a problem. Never refer a guest to someone else (like the manager). They have chosen to come to you for a reason. If they wanted the manager, they would have asked for the manager. The guest needs to feel that the person they are speaking to is the face of the company in that moment.

Empathize

Think about yourself in the same situation; how would you like to be treated? There is almost nothing your guest has experienced that you have not been through. Try to remember how you felt when a similar situation happened to you. My favorite response is, "I'm terribly sorry that this has happened to you. It must have been very frustrating." Or, "I am sorry this happened to you. I am going to work hard to correct the situation." It doesn't matter if the guest is wrong, mistaken, or completely unreasonable, the fastest way to diffuse a potentially explosive situation is by saying, and "I apologize for your experience."

Let's face it, even when guests are wrong, we can still regret that they had a bad experience. Apologizing tells the guest that you are taking responsibility for their satisfaction even if you cannot take responsibility for the wrong they think you have done. Some companies have adopted a strategy in which they actually ask if the customer will forgive them for letting them down before taking steps to resolve their complaint.

Ask

The best way to diffuse the emotions of a guest who has had a bad experience is to ask the appropriate questions and listen to their response. Get to the service gap so you can provide the appropriate recovery.

Solve

Once you understand the situation, apply the right response. Avoid citing company policy or offering an excuse for the error. Get to how you plan to help the guest. Give the guest two options when possible: "We can refund your money or exchange that jacket for another one." If you're not sure what to do, you can ask the guest, "What can I do to make this right?" Chances are, they will provide a simple solution that will satisfy their needs. If your team members are not empowered to handle guest concerns and complaints, the battle is lost long before it even begins. Delaying the fix or forcing team members to find someone else to fix the problem does not instill confidence in them and ultimately frustrates the guest. Fix it.

This goes without saying, but I will say it anyway. Fix the problem. But before fixing it, the team member should review with the guest what the concern was and what steps they are planning to take to address. This does two things: First, it checks for understanding, and second, it ensures that the planned fix is enough to satisfy the customer. For example, if the customer is a hotel guest who has just discovered their bathroom is dirty, will they be happy with a housekeeper coming up to clean it? If there was dust on the floor, perhaps. If the floor was flooded with smelly water, they might want a new room. It is important to clarify that what you consider a "fix" meets the customer's expectations.

Extra

Here is that critical opportunity you have to do more than expected. This final step in service recovery is the cement. Woodworkers will tell you that a beautiful piece of wooden furniture can be carefully crafted and perfectly stained. But if that piece is not painted over with a sealant, weather and time will undo all of the good work they have done. Yes, this extra step will probably cost you something. But the benefit is that it seals more than just the wooden furniture, it seals the customer experience for a long time to come.

In my restaurant, we had a specialty dessert that was only served to customers as part of the recovery effort. They were impressed to receive a special treat that is not on the menu and is being offered to them exclusively. I have also worked with retail companies that offered a small sample pack of a product. One big box store I know of has specific recovery coupons that were good for 10% off the customer's next purchase.

However, it is important not to break the bank in the recovery process. You have to know the point at which the recovery measure that would impress the guest outweighs the loss. In that case, you will have to try to negotiate a solution that will make them happy.

> "The focus of entertaining is impressing others; the focus of true hospitality is serving others."
>
> *Tim Chester*

Service recovery is a big part of any hospitality program. It needs to be a constant part of ongoing training and a regular subject in daily huddles. Practice makes perfect and could take a challenging situation and turn it around into a customer for life!

My role typically has me on the road over 300 days a year. I don't love travel, but I love what I do, so it's totally worth it. There is one thing I have learned to enjoy, and that is the status that all of this traveling gets me: room upgrades, free beverages, access to airport lounges, and the like. At some point, you become jaded and think you have seen it all. Then something happens that just blows you away, and that is where Alex comes in.

I was in the midst of a heavy travel month, going from city to city and place to place. It's the kind of week where everything starts to blend together and can take the humanity out of the experience. During this particular week, one of my flights was severely delayed, and I ended up reaching my hotel at 1 a.m. I approached the front desk, and as soon as I gave them my name, it was clear that something was wrong. They were over-sold and had given away my room! Of course I took out my platinum status card and pushed back. How could they have given away *my* room? I have this card that says I am important! To their credit, they got to work immediately. They assured me that they would find me a room at a really nice property close by, and that they would cover any additional expenses.

So we load my bags in the hotel shuttle and head out. Though it was dark when we pulled up to the hotel, I was pleasantly surprised and could tell that it was a very nice property. It was one of those really sleek boutique hotels with a cool bistro attached. When I walked to the front desk to check in, I noticed that there were a bunch of small aquariums with fish behind the front desk; not a typical sight, but pretty cool. I checked in, grabbed my bags, and started to head to the elevator. All of the sudden, the young lady at the desk stopped me.

"Mr. Fiato, can we get you a fish?" she said. "Excuse me?" I replied. "Mr. Fiato, we are a pet-friendly hotel and we noticed you didn't bring any pets. Would you like a fish for your room? We have one here for you named Alex."

It's now 3 a.m. and I am confused and intrigued. "Sure, I will take Alex," I replied. Sure enough, they brought Alex the fish to my room. They placed Alex on the desk with some food and directions on how to care for him during my stay.

Traveling can be lonely, boring, and uneventful, but not this time. In fact, I must say I loved my time with Alex! While working, I spoke to him, ran some ideas by him, and we even had room service together (he ate fish flakes). All around, it was a really unique experience that turned a tough week into something really special.

By the end of my stay, I must say that I would miss Alex and this really cool property. As I checked out, my phone went off. I figured this was my bill and I was curious as to what Hilton had to pay to put me up. Well to my surprise, it was not my bill, but instead it was a note from Alex the fish! Alex said he enjoyed staying with me and that if I was ever in town again and wanted to stay with him, they would match any other hotel's price. Wow, what a surprise! The next time I was in town, I took Alex up on his offer. When I got up to my room, who do you think was there waiting for me? Yep, it was Alex (I am not 100% sure it was the same fish, but I'll take it).

All in all, the hospitality I received was well worth missing out on the points. Well done!

Chapter 8

Developing a Dynamic Team

The greatest gift you can give yourself is a dynamic team. Put the time in to choose the right people. One of my favorite movies is "Miracle," as I am particularly fond of Kurt Russel's portrayal of Legendary Coach, Herb Brooks. In an early scene, Herb faced questions about the team he had selected. His colleagues felt that he left out some of the most skilled

> "Coming together is a beginning, staying together is progress, and working together is success."
>
> *Henry Ford*

players. Herb's response was simply, "I am not looking for the best players, I am looking for the right ones." History shows that Herb choose wisely, and his young team pulled off the greatest upset in sports history, ultimately winning the gold medal. Follow these steps to choose and develop your team:

1. *Your team must be diverse.*

Diversity of thought, diversity of abilities, and diversity of experience provides you with a deep bench that is able to respond to a bevy of challenges and creates an interesting mix of ideas and attitudes. Team diversity inspires positive conflict and ultimately results in out-of-the-box solutions.

Many companies conduct personality tests during the hiring process. I endorse this and highly recommend that you use these tests to create a diverse team. Different thinking and working styles help aid you in creating an effective team. It is important that everyone is aware of the pros and cons of their work styles so that they are mindful of their effect on the team. For you as the leader, your mission (should you choose to accept it) is to get to know your team. What are their interests, passions, and skills? When you match expertise and interest to tasks, you will have a more engaged team member who will then have a direct impact on the overall performance of the team. I once heard of a manager for the luxury brand, Lincoln, who would take three employees out to lunch each week. Together, they would sit and talk about their lives. No business talk was allowed. It was just an opportunity for the manager to get to know them and for them to get to know each other. The employees loved it and couldn't wait to get their chance to hang out with the manager and enjoy a fancy meal together. By understanding the employees on a personal level and knowing more about their personalities and passions, the culture of the team ran deep and the employees felt that they were better understood as human beings and not just names on the payroll.

2. *Value and reward collaboration.*

Make a point to recognize and value team members when they work together. Encourage each person to understand the strengths of other team members and how to leverage them as a team. The right way to do this is by recognizing each team member's strengths. The wrong way is to compare people. Everyone is bringing something different to the team dynamic and all of it is valuable. Making comparisons between people communicates that you don't value one or the other. It belittles one person's contribution. But even a small contribution is important. In one tech team, a member of the team did not speak often in meetings. She was the quiet sort. She often baked cookies and brought them to the office. People would gather around her desk, eat cookies, and brainstorm. The interesting thing about that is that it all happened by accident. Her desk became the most powerful and important location in the office. People loved to talk to her. She was great to bounce ideas off of. She asked the right questions that seemed to get people thinking. And, she was great at recognizing the impact an idea would have on another department. So, she would get on the phone, call someone from that department, and invite them up for cookies. The CEO of that company estimated that her desk (and her cookies) were responsible for millions of dollars of sales.

3. Act quickly to address problems.

Little is more frustrating than an impotent leader who lets problems fester until they bubble over into full-blown conflict. High-performance teams have managers who deal with issues promptly. Good leaders address issues quickly, but great leaders encourage people to resolve their own differences, only stepping in if and when no resolution is found. As you address problems, show no partiality. Your ability to deal with the situation, rather than the people, inspires trust and loyalty and fosters honest and open interaction between the people involved in the conflict.

4. Show loyalty toward the team.

Success is always shared, and it's important that you as the leader take the blame for failure. Take responsibility as a manager when things go wrong. For example, if there are customer issues or missed deadlines, own it, then coach and correct behaviors quickly. You are the leader, standing behind your team will create a feeling of connection. This is where your questioning skills become very useful. Let's take an issue and think it through:

Problem: A large meeting room was double booked.
Ask: Why was the room double booked?
Answer: Two reservationists were talking to potential guests at the same time about the same room.

Ask: Why were two reservationists talking to potential guests at the same time about the same room?
Answer: There is no system for holding a room when you are in negotiations with a potential client.

Ask: Why is there no system for holding a room?
Answer: We have never considered the possibility that such a thing could happen.

By asking the right questions, a solution can be implemented without anger, accusation, or reprimand. If you find yourself in a situation where poor performance needs to be addressed, it can still be done in a way that is positive and effective. When delivering feedback, stick to the facts, do not make it personal, and think about the benefits to the team. As the leader, you must guide the conversation toward the future. It's your job to remove barriers and company politics so the team can focus on solutions.

5. *Consistently hold conversations with direct reports with the intention to guide and provide feedback.*

Consistent communication is a key skill for leaders. The era of the yearly evaluation is thankfully coming to an end. A better technique is to engage in continual conversation with the team. Don't micromanage, but stay connected. This can be challenging in a busy hospitality environment. But the cost of not making time to do it is too heavy of a price to pay. So, find the time. Schedule it so that it will not be missed. Take time every day to walk the floor and talk to the team. Congratulate, celebrate, assist, coach, and care. And watch your team flourish. Managing from your office or the phone will bring you mediocrity.

6. *Define the goal.*

One amazing step you can take in your management paradigm is to commit to always being clear on what success looks like. Define the finish line. No runner would run a race without knowing where the finish line is. When the end zone is blurry, or worse, constantly moving, the team gets disoriented and unmotivated. As the leader, you should clearly explain to the team what success in any given project looks like. It is essential that you make the goal clear and vivid so the entire team shares the vision of success. The Pareto Principle states that 80% of the work gets done in 20% of the time. As your team gets closer to the goal, their efforts will intensify. They might walk toward the goal, but they will sprint toward the finish line. Don't forget to check for understanding. Use your knowledge of your team and effective communication skills to ensure everyone is clear about the objective.

7. Set a game plan.

Identify who will do what and how the team will work together. This staves off conflicts before they happen. Communicate the game plan by using a concept called framing, which simply means to lead by setting the direction for a project. In other words, you can help your team visualize how to start, provide guidance on the key collaborations that may be needed, and ultimately map out where the finish line is. Framing helps people know what success looks like so that they will know when they have achieved it.

Framing is a simple concept, but it can get a bit complex when you want to put it into action. At that point, it can get difficult because it forces you to walk the tightrope as a leader. You want to set direction and you want to point your team down a path, but you don't want to micromanage the process, which has the danger of stifling creativity and the diversity of ideas. You want your team to have room to use their skills to collaborate and to innovate. But you want quality work to get done within a specified range of time. It's a space that can feel as thin as a spider's eyelash. But just to put it in context, you should consider some of the many different management styles you can subscribe to. Let's explore them together.

Micromanagers

We have all worked with leaders who dictate the beginning, middle, and end of a project. They tell you what to do and exactly how to do it.

Then, they stand over you (literally or metaphorically) until you complete it. Sadly, even after you complete the project under their strict supervision, you will find that they are still unhappy. Here's the rub: no one identifies himself or herself as a micromanager. They live in a constant state of denial. A few quick questions can help you determine if you have fall under this management style. Remember, micromanagers are not leaders. So if you do see yourself in this test, run (don't walk) to the nearest therapist! Only kidding. Micromanaging, like any other issue, can be corrected. So here we go. You know you are a micromanager if you:

- Feel you have to make all of the important decisions
- Feel uncomfortable delegating work to others
- Check in with people frequently over the course of a week about their assignment
- See your role as controlling the quality of others' work
- Give orders more than you ask questions (this includes asking questions in an ordering tone as in, "Why the hell did you do that?")
- Are addicted to your to-do list
- Hold multiple meetings about the same issue to get updates
- Give your employees assignments with step-by-step instructions about how to do it
- Take tasks away from employees so that you can do it yourself

We all have felt the frustration and lack of creativity micromanaging can create. If you are a micromanager, it is hard for you to trust. The cure to micromanaging is to take baby steps. You will find that you easily revert to your old habits of control. So, you must be intentional. Give a smart and trusted employee a simple task and do not check in on them even once. Let them carry the ball to the goal line. Even if they fail, do not take the job from them. Find out if they have any questions and then express trust in them to take another run at it. And if you find that your employees aren't carrying their weight without the extra supervision, then they probably aren't a good fit for your team in the first place.

Visionaries

Visionaries provide another side of the coin. They are super creative, but lack the ability to explain what they want. They are always flying at 35,000 feet while the rest of us are on the ground looking up at them trying to see what they see. From that far away, we cannot hear them or understand what they want. Visionaries cause projects to stop and start and really struggle to reach completion. Because they are so distant, they don't seem to have an accurate appreciation for the execution phase of their grand plan.

Framers

Take the best of micromanagers and visionaries and combine them into one powerful leadership style, Framers. I personally use a simple five-step process to frame a project for my team. Here's how it looks:

Step 1: Clearly explain the project and provide all of the key points and milestones that the team will need. In my current role, my team supports the field consisting of frontline managers and team members. I always incorporate leadership and operations in the project from beginning to end. My team engages a leadership sponsor and a group of operators to collaborate with, which has helped us deliver a lot of successful projects.

Step 2: Set up a communication cadence. Have the team set meetings with you to cover progress on each of the pre-determined milestones and interactions. These communications are key and should never be rushed. It's important for you to visualize the direction the team is taking so that your feedback is constructive. It's at this point where leaders should fight the urge to micromanage the project, while still keeping the team focused on the goals, milestones, and timeline. My team knows that they can come to me at any time with concerns, but they do not have to worry about me breathing down their necks to ensure they are performing well or on task. They know that I trust them, and I trust that my hiring process has sifted out anyone who doesn't belong in my group. If they are on my team, it is because they know how to get the job done. They simply need me to define success, check in at predetermined times, and then get out of the way.

Step 3: At the halfway point, set up an update or a check-in with leadership or stakeholders. The idea is for the team as a whole, along with operational sponsors, to present progress to the senior leadership team. These sessions are designed to be interactive to ensure leadership has space to provide feedback.

Step 4: At this point, engage in 'reframing' where the feedback from the presentation to leadership is utilized to reframe the project. Now that the team has touched base with the stakeholders, they can look at the project to make sure all of the prior objectives are aligned with their needs, and they can ensure that they are on the path toward success. This is a great time to recognize the team's efforts, celebrate the innovation, and acknowledge the gaps. Most importantly, circle back to Step 1 to reset key points and milestones, and ensure the project is delivered on time.

Step 5: Once completed, allow the team to deliver their results. I personally do this because I want them to receive credit for the hard work and time they have put in.

Framing is such a critical team dynamic. More times than I can count, my team has delivered solutions that were much better than what I had envisioned. It always makes me think of the song "Hold on Loosely but Don't Let Go" by 38 Special. It's about giving your team both roots and wings. Roots keep your team grounded to the specifications of the project. Wings allow them to soar, test their limits, and try new things.

8. Ensure everyone clearly understands what needs to be done.

Be positive and enthusiastic in your belief that the team will succeed. Then, tell your team how much you trust and appreciate them. The ultimate solution the team delivers will be flawless and delivered on time 99.9% of the time. And even in that .01% where it isn't, the team will do everything in their power so that they do not disappoint you. This is the benefit of showing people that they are important to you. It has been said, "People don't care how much you know until they know how much you care." Once you have their hearts, they will freely offer their hands to get the job done.

Now that the team is excited and engaged, always check for understanding and have each team member recite back to you what they are responsible for and explain how they will work together. Always match a team member's skill using their strengths, weaknesses, and interest to a task as this will promote teamwork and participation. To move the team in the right direction and create a clear plan, answer the following questions before communicating with them.

Why are we doing this?
When do we need to finish the job?
How do we work together to drive results?

Who is responsible for which tasks?
What does success look like?

Seven years ago, I was in Atlanta conducting hospitality training. It was a small pharmaceutical company with about 1,000 employees on-site. I will never forget my first day there, one associate really stood out. She was out front talking to all of our guests, orchestrating service. I thought for sure she must be the manager, but she wasn't, her name was Helinda and she was a cashier.

Helinda has never had a bad day at work, ever. But today was different. All of her guests and her team members were asking her what was wrong, but she wouldn't say. It finally got so bad that our client called the manager and said, "Please get Helinda into the office and find out what is bothering her. She is upset and everyone is really worried about her." For seven years, she was the picture of hospitality and her team and guests loved her.

The manager brought her into the office and asked what was wrong. Helinda began to cry. She explained that her car was stolen, and as a single mother, she had no insurance on her car to replace it. In addition, she looked into public transportation and there were no busses that had a route that she could take to work. She took her keys from her pocket and said, "Today is my last day. I can't work here anymore." The manager asked Helinda to wait and that he would see what he could do to help her. So Helinda went back to work and the manager called our client to let him know the situation.

As a company, we went to work to help Helinda, but her guests went to work much faster. Within two hours, the company's CEO was in our café looking for Helinda. He pointed at her and said, "You're not leaving! We just had a meeting about you, and we decided to have a cab pick you up for work every day, and we will have that same cab bring you home every day. We will pay for this until you get this car thing straightened out." Helinda began to cry even more as she was blown away by the surprise gesture of kindness.

The CEO added, "Helinda, you have taken care of us for seven years, let us take care of you for a while. I want you to meet the cab driver to make sure you two are good with each other."

Together, they walked down the hall, down the stairs, and outside. But when she went outside, all 1,000 employees were there waiting for her. But there was no cab in sight, they had bought a car for her!

> "Customer service shouldn't just be a department, it should be the entire company."
>
> Tony Hsieh

So anytime you think what you do is not important, I would tell you to think again. Any time you think you don't have an influence on your guest's lives, I would say you're wrong. It's a choice that you make every day when you come to work. Helinda chose to embrace her guests and have a positive role in their work lives. And when she needed them, they were there for her.

I can't promise you that you will get a car, but I can promise you that this is the very best way to approach your work life.

Leading and inspiring highly effective teams is a rewarding endeavor. There is nothing more satisfying than catching your team representing your company and brand with excellence, creativity, and energy. It is the essence of what comprises hospitality. But far too many leaders are managing teams that are woefully unmotivated and disengaged. The old and ineffective strategy for dealing with underperformance has been to double down on futile management tactics that demotivate the team and drive employee turnover. As some managers like to say, "Firings will continue until morale improves." This speaks to such a manager's inability to understand that browbeating employees into submission only decreases productivity.

In a Harvard Business Review article, authors Robert Quinn and Anjan Thakor wrote:

"Employees choose to respond primarily to the incentives outlined in their contracts and the controls imposed on them. Consequently, they not only fail to see opportunities but also experience conflict, resist feedback, underperform, and personally stagnate. So managers, believing that their assumptions about employees have been validated, exert still more control and rely even more heavily on extrinsic

incentives. Employees then narrowly focus on achieving those rewards, typically at the expense of activities that are hard to measure and often ignored, such as mentoring subordinates and sharing best practices. Overarching values and goals become empty words. People do only what they have to do. Results again fall short of expectations, and managers clamp down further."

So what are managers to do when they want to improve their teams' work experience, delight and amaze their guests, build their brands, increase customer loyalty, and upsurge their profits? I have a few ideas and stories to help you figure it out.

The Keys to Leading a Team

A consistently sold-out hotel, filled reservation book, and positive customer reviews are great indicators of a business model that values employees and understands the importance of exceptional

> "If you want to go fast, go alone. If you want to go far, go together."
>
> *African Proverb*

hospitality. It is a worthy ideal to strive for, but make no mistake, getting there will not happen accidentally. Intentional leadership with a clear focus on hospitality is the only path toward highly inspired and productive teams that delight and astonish your clientele. The following are the foundational principles that result in these "super teams." Each one is massively impactful on its own. But when they are combined, the force of their effectiveness is unmatched.

Principle #1: Establish purpose, values, and behaviors.

Companies, similar to humans, are living, breathing organisms. They experience birth, growth, sickness, health, aging, and death. Humans search for purpose, and live by a set of values and functions based on a system of behaviors. Organizations must first have a purpose. This purpose is not simply what we do, it is more why we exist. Understand your responsibility in the performance cycle of each team member and why this is important in building a high-performance team. Purpose might easily be the single most critical aspect driving the way people and companies function. All companies develop mission statements, but they are almost always weak, pedantic, or vague. The mission statement, statement of purpose, or values statement should be written with extreme care to reflect the heart of the company's vision in clear and concise language. Once the company's purpose has been established, it becomes easy to craft a set of core values by which it will operate, which leads to the dependably positive behaviors by both management and the frontline team.

In an Inc.com article, author Minda Zetlin highlights some of the worst mission statements of all time. One company's reads: Our worldwide operations are aligned around a global strategy called the

Plan to Win, which centers on an exceptional customer experience--People, Products, Place, Price and Promotion. Think about if you were an associate at this company; would you feel like you understood your shared purpose? If your team cannot connect with your mission, you lose. If your team cannot visualize their role in your strategy, you lose. So instead of creating your mission statement in a home office that's far away from the field, get the operators involved. A mission crafted with very team you want to execute it is a recipe for success.

Principle #2: Demonstrate the highly effective behaviors and habits of a team leader.

Leadership by example is an often misunderstood concept. I will try to unpack it now in a way that is actionable for you in your day-to-day operations by first exploring what it is not. It is not simply talking about the right behaviors and attitudes. It is not about signage or branding. It is not about evaluating your employees when they meet or fail to meet the standard you have set. All of those are important to implement. But the concept of demonstrating highly effective behaviors lies in the ability to live the behaviors you expect from your team. It starts with you. If you demand qualities from your team that you are not willing (or able) to display, you cannot expect your team to rise to those higher levels. How you treat your team, your colleagues, your superiors, and most importantly, your customers, will speak louder than anything you say or write in an email. As the old saying goes, "As the head goes, so goes the body." The way a team works together is a reflection of YOUR leadership style and abilities. If you see dissention, division, and disrespect among your team members, it is very likely a result of some failing on your part to communicate those high order values we explored in principle one. It is up to managers and owners to set the tone, which ultimately sets the culture for the business. By setting this tone and plotting this course in no uncertain terms, you can hold your team accountable to work under the values you identify as the hallmark of your corporate philosophy. This builds positive teamwork.

A manager for a large global corporation said, "I do not require anything of my employees that I do not demonstrate to them in my own actions. If I ask them to show up early with a positive attitude, I can't go golfing, show up when I feel like it, and walk in grumpy because I had a bad game."

> "People are dying to work for great leaders. They want to be part of an engaged and successful team. They want to have fun, learn, grow and be rewarded for their contributions. The only question is, will they find that in your team or will they have to look elsewhere?"
>
> *Jack Welch*

Principle #3: Set an expectation of high performance and extreme integrity.

Nothing can destroy morale and decimate engagement faster than a culture of unfairness. Managers who appear to be duplicitous or who engage in favoritism and corporate nepotism will have a hard time getting the rest of the team to trust them. Be fair and ethical in everything you do. This will accomplish two very important goals:

1. **It will make it easy to work for you.**

People appreciate knowing exactly where they stand. When the ground beneath them is steady and solid, they come to work every day feeling secure in their position. They know how their efforts fit into the overall vision and purpose of the company.

2. **It will make it challenging to work for you.**

People don't quit companies. They quit bosses or jobs. Either they dislike what they do, or they dislike who they have to work for. One study found that more than 50% of people surveyed said they would rather have more fulfilling work than a pay raise. Setting high expectations is actually extremely motivating. It communicates a high level of trust. It speaks to your belief in their competence. The added bonus is that it is good for the company's financial health. Studies show that higher levels of employee satisfaction can result in double digit increases in profits on the bottom line.

Set clear and challenging goals for your team. Give them something of value to strive for. And constantly communicate your belief in their ability to get the job done. In such a culture, you will see productivity, creativity, and hospitality soar.

Principle #4: Inspire participation, collaboration, and celebration.

Understand that any employee could interact with any guest at any time. A guest could stop a maintenance professional in the middle of changing out light bulbs just to ask a question. Every employee in every department should be made to feel as part of the winning team.

You can inspire participation by setting goals, but these goals should not thunder down from the mountain of Zeus. They should be developed in concert with the team that will be expected to reach them. Allowing people to set their own goals has amazing results. People are more engaged when they set the goal, and their likelihood of achieving the goal increases. Furthermore, people are more likely to set far more challenging goals for themselves than you might set for them. Once a project has started in conjunction with the team, create daily, measurable goals for them. The goals must have clear accountability, expectations, and a deadline. Create an environment where team and individual goals can be discussed as you offer the support they will need to get them done.

The employees at the Ritz-Carlton could never have crafted such an amazing guest experience for Joshie's family if their management did not give them the time, flexibility, and resources to do so. Would you have thought to pose the toy around the hotel having an extended vacation to give the little boy comfort that Joshie was happy and safe? I probably wouldn't have. But some ingenious employee thought of that and enlisted the help of the rest of the team to make it happen. That is the level of collaboration that can be established anywhere!

Celebration is the final step in the trifecta. Celebrate anything and everything. Recognition is another one of those magic wands that seems to boost productivity and creativity in any organization. As your team is working to amaze and surprise your customers, you should be working to amaze and surprise your team when they achieve. Take every opportunity to celebrate successes because doing so will improve process and results. The team will feed you better and better ideas about how to deliver exceptional hospitality, and you will thank them with better and better recognition responses. It becomes a thriving cycle of rewards for everyone involved.

Be inclusive and invite other departments' input in projects. Expose your team to other players in the organization. Consider it a success when a member of your team is chosen for a promotion or a move to another group. It's a positive reflection on you as a leader, on your team, and the culture you have created.

Principle #5: Coach your team through the process.

One of the areas you can work in is your ability to coach the team. Paying attention to your team's individuality will help you to identify the unique ways in which each member can contribute to elevating the level of hospitality delivered. It's a technique with a fantastic side effect: people appreciate that you recognize their special talents and they want to give even more of themselves to impress you. As you help them develop those special skills, you foster a sense of loyalty in them.

Coaching is not a one-way street where you rely only on your ability to teach and train the team. It also involves receiving from the team by asking questions that let them express concerns, offer ideas, and provide insight into what is going on in the frontline activities they perform each day. Believe it or not, they know your business better than you do. Their perspectives are a gold mine. To encourage team participation, use your coaching skills. Great leaders ask more questions than they make statements, and they consistently challenge the team to bring results forward. This will encourage your team to work together, which inevitably builds team morale.

Leadership is a huge opportunity to not only grow personally, but it also gives you the ability to reach out and pull others up. As the team leader, you set the tone for your team, leading by example using the five principles listed above. As you grow as a leader, you will gain respect, buy-in, and build your team's confidence.

To build positive teamwork, focus on the end result you are trying to achieve. An example of this is to assign tasks for the day to individual members of the team, then focus on the completion of those tasks as a team versus the individual who completed them. Timely completion of tasks as a team is far more important than who completed them.

Chapter 9
Collaboration and Accountability

One of my favorite examples of accountability comes from the time I spent at the Seattle Fish Market. After reading "Fish," I spent three days at the market observing the fishmongers delight guests with their high energy approach to guest service. During slow times, I would interact with the guys, trying to learn and find nuggets I could bring back to my team. A fishmonger named Bear talked to me about accountability. He explained that they owed it to each other to "choose their attitude" prior to arriving to work. The show that they put on every day was totally dependent on the entire team's focus on "playing" with the guests in order to "make their day."

That made sense to me, so I asked the obvious question, "What happens if you have a bad day? What happens if you come to work in the wrong mindset?" His answer was simple, "There is plenty of work to do out back." Meaning simply, if you come to work in a foul mood, you don't work out front, you don't interact with guests, and you don't get to mess with the team's chemistry. You work out back. They hold you accountable to the rules they mutually agreed upon:

- Choose your attitude
- Play according to the rules
- Be present
- Make the guests' day

Teamwork requires two critical elements: accountability and collaboration. Together, they serve as the fuel that powers highly effective teams. Being a leader is the art of completing work through others. It is both a science and an art. But in order for the team to function well, you must instill the two traits. We will begin with accountability.

> "Unity is strength...when there is teamwork and collaboration, wonderful things can be achieved."
>
> Mattie J.T. Stepanek

Accountability: Be Consistent

The first step in asking your team to be accountable is to be accountable to them. That means that you must be consistent. Nothing frustrates team members more than a leader who can't make up his or her mind. When you say something to them, be sure you can deliver. Then you can hold everyone accountable to what they committed to.

Accountability is the fuel that powers highly effective teams. Your team will appreciate that you hold yourself to a high standard, and they will respect that you hold everyone to one single standard—without playing favorites or making broad exceptions. Accountability ensures everyone is working equally. If you allow a team member to slide—to do less than others—it will erode your team's confidence in you. Accountability ensures equal distribution of work and the expectation that all tasks will be completed on time.

In addition to accountability, you need to set high expectations of the work that is completed. As a leader, you cannot settle for work that is sub-par. Constantly challenge your team to deliver work using the latest and greatest platforms. Reward "outside the box" solutions and those team members who invest time mastering platforms with efficient and effective solutions. As a leader, you need innovation and that need should translate throughout the team. This will eliminate any chance that your team becomes complacent, because once this happens, the team will soon become irrelevant. Morale will dip, customers will notice, and sales will drop. It is the leader's job to make sure that never happens.

Accountability: Performance Management

Performance management requires collaboration, accountability, and consistency. Team members will only reach their full potential if you take responsibility for managing their performance. Performance management is a cycle that allows you and your team members the opportunity to review accomplishments, set objectives, and establish development plans.

Performance management is not a start and finish cycle, but a continuous conversation that takes place throughout an employees' career. Take advantage of every opportunity, both positive and negative, to coach your team. As a leader, you must constantly nudge your team to bring the best version of themselves to work every day. Elements of strong performance management include:

1. *Performance planning*

    Setting and communicating expectations mutually; establishing clear, realistic, and measurable performance objectives; defining measures of success

2. *Development planning*

    Assessing strengths and areas for growth determine the next steps for training and development to grow your team members' skills. Investing in team training is critical to a team's success.

3. *Evaluation and providing feedback*

    Discussing progress and celebrating success is not a once a year activity! Coaching occurs daily

4. *Performance assessment*

Evaluating performance; celebrating accomplishments; Discussions on improvement and rewarding performance against objectives.

Collaboration: Create a Vision

The second part of our duo of inspiration is that of collaboration. To inspire collaboration and cooperation, you must understand that it is a spirit of cooperation that you are seeking. You are hoping to develop an attitude rather than behaviors. Part of this is ensuring that you value all of the contributions of the team. Even the ideas that are not implemented should be celebrated. This helps to draw out and celebrate the diversity of the team and fosters innovating thinking.

One powerful way to inspire collaboration is to paint a clear and compelling vision for the team. When your team knows the causes behind the decisions that are made or the policies that are put in place, they are far more willing to buy in to them. And, speaking of buy-in, it is easier to obtain when the team is involved in setting goals and planning policy. Decisions that come from faceless executives at the top of the chain might inspire obedience, but it does not engender collaboration.

In a Forbes magazine article, Leadership Strategist Carol Kinsey Giman, writes:

"Collaboration is also intrinsically inspiring because it has an emotional payoff. People like being part of a winning team, and as one collaborative leader told me: "There is a phenomenal sense of accomplishment in achieving as a group what could never have been achieved as individuals."

Trust starts with you; your team needs to count on what you say. Your commitment to fairness and a high ethical standard is your best tool. Think before you speak, communicate openly, honestly, and often. Encourage open discussion, listen respectfully, and above all else, keep your word and walk the talk. You also need to be aware when conversations need to end, direction needs to be set, and the group needs to be empowered to lead.

When delegating, ensure you distribute the work evenly, especially the undesirable tasks that nobody enjoys doing. Make every effort not to play favorites. People will notice and inequity will build resentment.

Ask questions instead of making assumptions

Believe it or not, it takes a lot of courage to ask questions, but it is fairly easy to make assumptions. We think we know what everyone else is thinking and what their motivations might be. So, we "think" for others and "speak for others" without ever really checking to be sure. Asking questions requires us to humble ourselves enough to say that we do not have all of the answers and that we want to hear the thoughts and opinions of others.

Delegate, delegate, delegate!

A strong component of collaboration and cooperation is delegation. It is a key skill, and by practicing the art of delegation, you will encourage team members to work together to complete tasks. In the end, they will feel rewarded and can celebrate success together. Here are a few ways to demonstrate delegating to your team:

- Ask for input and decision making in the planning process.
- Spread the more enjoyable tasks around.
- Ask for volunteers; Interest is great a motivator.
- Assign a team member whose talent and interests fit the need.

Your team is a micro culture; it's a small part of a larger company. Collaboration and accountability are the guardrails. You must do everything you can to keep your team from working in a silo. I encourage my team to interact, collaborate, and work with all departments. In fact, it has become part of our process. We loop in everyone so there are no surprises. This dynamic has elevated my teams profile throughout the organization. It's also become reciprocal as other teams constantly reach out to us and involve us in projects. The ultimate win-win.

Conclusion

The power of hospitality cannot be overstated or exaggerated. It is the difference between long-term success and immediate failure. Particularly in our current culture where people are more internally focused, your efforts toward creating a culture of hospitality will be richly rewarded by your guests. I will end by summarizing some of my best tips for ensuring great cultural experiences:

Create a rewarding culture

Creating an environment that inspires great service is everyone's job. Rewarding and

> "Hospitality workers become family to each other. You look to your left and your right and say, 'That's somebody I can learn from; that's somebody I can have fun with; that's somebody I want to be a champion with and be the best at what we do.' I don't think there is anything I am prouder of than the quality of human beings who work here."
>
> *Danny Meyer, Union Square Hospitality Group*

recognizing achievers is the backbone to every hospitality-based culture.

The 80x20 rule

Most managers spend 80% of their time with the bottom 20% of their team. I am asking you to try inverting that equation. The very best way to drive your culture is to provide leadership and attention to your top performers. Celebrate them, reward them, and acknowledge them. It creates a culture that celebrates achievers and really has no room for mediocrity or average performance.

The Platinum Rule:

Finally, for you leaders out there, everything we covered in this book comes back to the way you should treat your team, thinking back to the platinum rule which states, "Do unto others as they would be done unto." Remember the mirror analogy. When you arrive on site, be intentional about smiling, making eye contact, and greeting all of your team members individually. Show up to work well-groomed and dressed perfectly to set the example. Be present with your team members in every interaction, making sure to actually spend time with them. Set goals every week that challenge your team and reward execution. At the end of each day, sincerely thank your team for all of their hard work.

Start again tomorrow

No matter what happens in any given day, you can start again tomorrow. Set your mistakes to the side. Do not put them behind you, because then you cannot see them and learn from them. But setting them to the side means that they are not in front of you as stumbling blocks, they are not behind you making you oblivious to them, but they are off to the side to refer to and improve upon day by day.

This final story has had a profound effect on me; I don't tell it often as I struggle to get through it. As I shared previously, I do a lot of live focus groups with guests. Every time I think I have heard it all, I am proven wrong.

On this day, I was at a large military contractor's site working on improving the guest experience for the second shift. The clients lined up one session after the other where we got a lot of great information and I was excited to share it with the operational team. My last session was at 10 p.m. and I was mentally and physically exhausted from the day.

The last group began to file in and a man in a wheelchair caught my eye. He looked very focused and really unhappy, so I prepared for the worst. To my surprise, he said nothing throughout the entire session, and instead just sat and stared. At the end of the session, the group filed out, except for the gentlemen in the wheelchair. It was clear that he had something to share and he wanted to do it without the other guests in the room. This is not unusual. In fact, it happens quiet often, and most of the time it's because the guest's complaint is personal in nature and has something to do with one of our team members. This was not that.

The gentleman's name was Dave and he had a story to tell. Dave was a proud Marine. By looking at him, I would guess that in his prime he was 6'6 in and 240 pounds, a physical specimen to be sure. But it was clear that the man in front of me was sick. A sickness that left him weak and thin.

When Dave retired from the Marines, he came to this location to work and he was in his 10th year with the company. Six months ago, during a routine physical, they found a lump on his neck, which turned out to be stage 4 cancer. His prognosis was not good. He told me about his treatments and the toll they took on his body and his mind. He explained that everyone he knew and everyone he worked with started to treat him differently. The worst part for him was that after treatments, he became so weak that he needed help to do the simplest of tasks. For this proud Marine, the combination of asking for help and the pity from his co-workers was more than he could take. I could see in his eyes that his situation had become very dark. He desperately needed a lifeline and it was at this point he started to tell me about the marketplace and Jessica.

Jessica was the cashier at this location's marketplace. As it turns out, both she and Dave had started working at this location around the same time. Dave was a twice a day guest who came in regularly for coffee in the morning and lunch every day. Needless to say, they were well acquainted. But Jessica became Dave's lifeline.

He explained that she was the only person who didn't distance herself from him. In fact, once he started treatments, she began meeting him at the marketplace entrance. He claimed he would wheel in and she would magically appear with a big smile and a greeting. Without asking, she would grab a tray and walk through the marketplace with him. Jessica would help get his food and drink. She would bring his meal to his usual spot and sit with him and have lunch. He explained that she did all of this in a way that just made him feel so normal. When he was well enough to come to work, he always looked forward to lunch with Jessica.

Then Dave started to get better! At the time of our interaction, he was in remission and felt confident of his future. He felt that he owed it all to Jessica and he wanted me to know that. It was clearly hard for him to share all of this with me, but he was on a mission.

Back at my hotel that night, I couldn't sleep. I was scheduled for a flight out first thing in the morning, but I couldn't go! I had to stay and meet Jessica.

I returned to the account the next morning and had coffee with Jessica. She is exactly what I expected: a wonderful, compassionate young lady who brought the best version of herself to work every day. She fully understood that what she did for work was important. She knew that she could have a positive effect on the lives of her guests and her team. I don't think she fully understood the effect she had on Dave. Hospitality was a natural state to Jessica, and it fueled her reaction to the situation.

These are my best days; the moments that I get to spend with the truly amazing people that are the frontline of our company. They inspire and motivate me to be a better person, and they have given me the hospitality edge.

Acknowledgements

I wanted to take a moment to recognize how lucky I am to work for a company like Compass group. I have been blessed with great opportunity and have met some amazing industry leaders.

At some point in their career, everyone has had someone who has helped move them forward. I want to take this opportunity to recognize those who have helped me, in order of when we have worked together.

Bruce Blake	Susie Weintraub
Rodney Adams Blake	Jordan Wolski
Dan Raycroft	Rick Jacobs
John Costello	Michael Svagdis
Eric Fox	John Valentine
Tom Ciarletta	Tom Teves
John Noble Masi	Mark H. Maloney
Kristi Johnson	Ed Mugnani
Joe Maher	Garwin Freeze
Rick Post	Tony McDonald

About the Author

Mike has a passion for hospitality and creating a workplace atmosphere that inspires great experiences for both teams and guests, with whom he spends the majority of his time in the field. He personally develops and delivers guest service training for thousands of frontline team members every year.

In addition, he has conducted focus groups with over 150,000 guests and has an in-depth understanding of consumers. A keen focus on generational preferences and business types has helped Mike drive guest loyalty and build same-store sales. As Eurest's Senior Vice President of Customer Experience, he works directly for the CEO and shares his consumer data and research with all Eurest support teams.

Mike is a graduate of the Disney Institute, Ritz Carlton training, and Zingerman's Service Training, and continues to seek out exceptional service. He lives in St Petersburg, Florida, with his wife and high school sweetheart, Kristen, where they actively participate in fostering animals that need a home.

www.ingramcontent.com/pod-product-compliance
Lightning Source LLC
Chambersburg PA
CBHW060845220526
45466CB00003B/1253